D

The Life and Legacy of Reginald Perrin

A Celebration

Richard Webber

Virgin

For Paula with love

Acknowledgements

This book would not have been possible without the help of so many people. My thanks to all the actors who generously gave up their time to talk to me. I am also grateful to their agents for putting me in touch, and to the staff of Spotlight and Equity for dealing with my endless stream of calls for contact numbers.

Gareth Gwenlan and John B Hobbs's help was equally as important: their memories have helped bring the book alive. Thanks also to Caren Williams, the production secretary; Ronnie Barker and Richard Briers for allowing me to publish their contributions; and Gillian Raine, Peter Bowles and David John for talking to me about Leonard.

This is the ideal opportunity to thank Hilary Johnson for all her help and guidance not just with this book, but in everything I have passed her way, and Rod Green and Lorna Russell at Virgin, whose enthusiasm for this project has been very welcome.

I would particularly like to thank David Nobbs and his agent Brie Burkeman. David's support from the book's inception has been paramount, without which this project would never have got off the ground. Many thanks also for writing the foreword.

Finally, I would like to thank Paula, my wife, for her constant love and support, as well as her patience whilst watching endless episodes of Reggie Perrin, and enduring my numerous telephone interviews during the research period.

First published in 1996 by
Virgin Books
an imprint of Virgin Publishing Ltd
332 Ladbroke Grove
London W10 5AH

ISBN 1 85227 686 X

Designed by Design 23, London
Printed and bound in Great Britain by Butler & Tanner Ltd, Frome and London

Contents

Foreword

BY DAVID NOBBS

When a vegetarian Indian restaurant with the splendid name of Veggie Perrin's opened in Plymouth last year, I felt that Reggie Perrin had received its ultimate accolade. After all, it had already been the subject of a question in Trivial Pursuit.

But all that pales beside a whole book on the subject. It is, of course, the only subject on which I am the world's leading authority, and therefore the only book to which I am ever likely to be asked to write the foreword.

I read the book with great interest, even the synopses of the scripts. I was amazed to find how much I'd forgotten! Nevertheless, its special interest for me lies in the incidental anecdotes, which have taken me straight back to the 1970s and in particular the magical hot summer of 1976, when it all began. I hope that these stories will give readers a real insight into the atmosphere and richness that went into what was a particularly happy experience.

I also found the biographies of the principal actors fascinating. One doesn't ask established actors, 'How did you begin your career? Tell me about the days when you were a nobody,' so there is much here that I didn't know even after making 28

programmes with them.

For instance, I had no idea that Bruce Bould had originally turned down the part of David Harris-Jones. The cheeky swine! How lucky for me, as well as for him, that he changed his mind. His is just one of the many superb performances for which I am deeply indebted.

It was only through Richard Webber's researches that I discovered, after I had sent Tony Webster to New Zealand, that Trevor Adams had returned to the business.

Richard Webber's book has given me sorrow as well as pleasure. In bringing Leonard Rossiter back to life he has re-awakened the sense of loss brought on by his untimely death, and I have been saddened also at the number of supporting artists who have died or suffered serious illness.

I'm constantly surprised to find how many Perrin fans there are in the world. When I give talks I have to be very careful as there are usually people there who know the books and programmes better than I. In fact, I may not be the world's leading authority even on this subject. I hope a great many of these fans buy this book and it will give them much pleasure.

Introduction

It is hard to believe two decades have passed since Reggie stripped off on a Dorset beach and ran into the sea for the opening credits of *The Fall and Rise of Reginald Perrin*. It is equally hard to believe that the angst-ridden suburbanite's entire adventures were packed into just 10.5 hours of classic British comedy.

In truth, Reggie Perrin has never been far away: constant repeats on both mainstream and satellite TV have kept the Perrin legend very much to the fore and have helped the well-loved series reach cult status, while David Nobbs's intrinsically funny novels continue to sell well.

Such is the influence of Nobbs's creation that it has even inspired the opening of Veggie Perrin's, a Plymouth-based vegetarian restaurant. Its walls are adorned with photos of the series, while its advertising slogan is 'I didn't get where I am today by eating meat!' When it first opened its doors in 1995, none other than John Barron was invited along to carry out the opening ceremony.

TV history is full of formulaic comedies with predictable plots and characters, but that could never be said of Reggie Perrin. So why has the legendary series remained fresh and accessible when many productions from the 70s have long since fallen into obscurity?

There are numerous reasons for its undisputed popularity. Reggie's circuitous life was depicted beautifully through Nobbs's clever and uproarious scripts. Not only did he write funny dialogue, but he also created strong and memorable characters, all of whom transferred well to the small screen.

Unlike many other sitcoms, one of Reggie Perrin's strengths was its endless supply of zany individuals which meant it did not rely solely on its main star to carry the show. No one could argue about Leonard Rossiter being the driving force throughout the three series – after all, he was playing the lead – but what was rare in comparison with the rest of the sitcom genre was the quality of the whole cast: supporting and minor members, all skilfully played and humorous in their own right.

The whole atmosphere associated with Reggie Perrin was convivial and professional. Its production was slick and crisp and the comedy oozed quality. Containing a laugh a line, and filmed at a breakneck speed, partly due to Leonard's rate of delivery, each episode developed its own identity.

But one of the main factors which has ensured the series' longevity is that the motivation behind each of the three series is timeless. In the first, the banality of Reggie's everyday existence as just another victim caught up in the monotony of life's treadmill struck a chord with countless people, many of whom could relate to his anxieties caused partly by the pressure, politics and pettiness of industry. But at least Reggie had the guts to try and do something about it even if his success was a little suspect. The other two series also concentrated on themes that remain just as apposite today.

The autumn of '96 will see the series resurrected. There will be much interest when the new seven-parter hits our screens without, of course, the skills of Leonard Rossiter. This time David has homed in on another social problem – the treatment of OAPs and the ever-present threat to job security – wrapped it in comedy and

produced another masterpiece in novel and script form.

Now is an apt moment to produce a Companion celebrating the Perrin legend. As an ardent fan of Reggie Perrin, one of my primary objectives in writing this book has been to provide for the first time as much information as anyone would ever need about the new series as well as the original three series, including details about how the programme came about; full cast interviews; complete synopsis of all 21 episodes and profiles of all the actors who played a part, regardless of magnitude.

I hope you enjoy reading it as much as I have enjoyed writing it.

RICHARD WEBBER
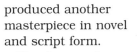
CLEVEDON - 1996

The Birth of Reginald Perrin

It is not often you find a writer who is actually pleased his work was rejected, but that is how author David Nobbs feels whenever he thinks back to a day in 1974 when a BBC producer turned down his idea for a play.

BBC Pebble Mill were planning a series of plays highlighting some of the social problems at that time, and David – after being asked to submit an idea – put forward a synopsis for a half-hour play about a man who goes barmy after being caught up in the rat race. The idea was rejected.

'The producer explained in his letter that he'd declined it because he was looking for problems affecting the modern world and didn't think my suggestion suitable,' says David. 'Because it was dressed up in comedy he failed to see the central theme of the play was both serious and topical.'

In hindsight, David Nobbs realises the rejection – albeit saddening at the time – marked the turning point in his writing career. 'As a writer you never waste a good idea so I sat down and turned my one-page synopsis into a novel which was to change my life from being a jobbing writer into a successful novelist. I was happy enough with what I'd achieved at that point in my career: I was writing regularly for The Two Ronnies, and had written three novels, but it was Reggie Perrin that established my name in the minds of the public.

Once completed, David's agent, Jonathan Clowes, sent the manuscript titled *The Death of Reginald Perrin* to Methuen, publishers of his previous three novels: *The Itinerant Lodger, A Piece of the Sky is Missing* and *Ostrich Country*. The reaction of the editor was mixed, as David recalls: 'He felt the first half of the book was very good, but the second half completely wrong, and when I thought about his comments I had to agree.'

In many ways, the Reggie Perrin saga was still at an embryonic stage and when his agent failed to obtain a commission from Methuen, David took the manuscript back to the drawing board. 'The story was completely different from what we now recognise as the first novel,' he explains, 'because Reggie ended up in a mental home.'

The revised second half of the novel introduced all the familiar scenes: Reggie running away; discarding his clothes on a Dorset beach; faking his own suicide, and returning to remarry his wife, Elizabeth. While his agent studied the redrafted text, David – convinced he had successfully addressed the book's original weaknesses – holidayed in Guernsey. Four days into his break, a telegram arrived from Jonathan Clowes. It read: 'I didn't get where I am today without knowing a good book when I see one. J.C.' David was chuffed. 'My agent's very shrewd and can spot things a mile off. He'd recognised one of the catchphrases that was to become famous in its own right.'

Upon David's return to England, his agent began sending the revised manuscript to publishers. Disappointed with Methuen's earlier rejection, Jonathan Clowes decided to try other publishers.

Eighteen publishers later, David and his agent's unremitting pertinacity paid dividends when publishers Victor Gollancz accepted the book. 'In many ways it was such a relief,' says David, 'because they accepted it as it was, appreciating my style of humour.'

When published in 1975, *The Death of Reginald Perrin* – later to become *The Fall and Rise of Reginald Perrin* – attracted favourable reviews and sold well. 'Obviously I was very pleased,' says David. 'I remember visiting the local John Lewis a few days after publication to buy some garden furniture. While I was there, I spotted a woman carrying a copy of my book under her arm; I felt like telling her I was the author but decided against it because it seemed a naff thing to do.'

When studying the intricate storyline running throughout the novel and subsequent TV series, one has to question whether any of the stresses or frustrations endured by Reggie originate not just from David Nobbs's vivid imagination, but from experiences in his own life. 'The themes are entirely invented and contain nothing that can be termed autobiographical,' claims David. 'I haven't worked in a factory, or for a food firm; I never had a boss like C.J. or met anyone who behaved like Reggie. What the story contains are my views on life in general, something I'd tested out in *A Piece of the Sky is Missing* – the novel preceding Reggie Perrin – about a man who hated working for a company so much that he reverted to such things as scribbling graffiti in the loos. He also rebelled against the company's management ethos which extended to the farcical idea of executive and non-executive toilets. I didn't realise it then, but the book was a dry run for Reggie Perrin.

David Nobbs believes there is a deep vein of silliness within the whole management culture of industry. 'Obviously I'm only an observer because I've never been involved in it myself, but there's evidence of this silliness wherever you go. For example, the country is littered with conference hotels where masses of people gather wearing little name tags informing others what job they do - to me, there seems a fair amount of farce in the whole thing.'

David's childhood was steeped in the world of the commuter, and these early observations were vital when developing the idea for his Reggie Perrin novels. 'I suppose the only autobiographical influence relates to my experience of growing up in Orpington, Kent,' he says. 'Each morning I caught the 8.14 from Orpington to my prep school, while my father caught the earlier 8.02 to Cannon Street. My train was always teeming with commuters and I spent the whole journey watching everyone with their briefcases, rolled umbrellas and bowler hats heading for the office. Even at that young age I hoped I would never end up like them.'

Around the vicinity of David's house, little streets and new estates provided homes for middle-class families - all very suburban and true commuter country. It was this world that later influenced his writing and helped create the edifice on which Reggie Perrin grew.

As for the name Reggie Perrin, David's not sure where the idea came from. 'I had already chosen the initials R.I.P because it seemed appropriate for a character seeking a better life, and who later faked his own suicide. But I'm not sure why I plumped for Reginald Iolanthe Perrin, other than Iolanthe struck me as a funny name.

'For my first holiday after series one had been transmitted, I travelled to France. While I was driving off the ferry, I noticed a lorry in front of my car had Perrins plastered all over the side of the trailer. Even more extraordinary is that in the first series there's a scene where Reggie goes to a restaurant and orders ravioli, followed by ravioli, followed by more ravioli. And while visiting Nice I spotted a factory called Perrins Ravioli!'

Adding to Reggie Perrin's mid-life crisis was the assemblage of characters he encountered, many of whom followed him through the various phases of his complicated existence. One reason for the novel and TV adaptation's success was the strength, depth and hilarity of these supporting characters, none of whom was

John Horsley as Doc Morrisey

based on anyone David had encountered before. Taking stock figures he added amusing idiosyncrasies until he reached the likes of C.J., Doc Morrisey and the rest of the gang.

With C.J. he tried creating the ultimate autocratic boss. He was always rattling out clichés incorrectly and loved playing with his executive toys adopted to inflate his self-importance. He bought farting chairs with the sole intention of humiliating his visitors and positioned them lower than his gigantic desk as a sign of superiority. 'I've sat in lots of chairs – particularly leather suites – that make noises as they release air, and thought it was ideal for C.J.,' explains David. 'Then I created David and Tony as a couple of yes-men, the sort of creeps you get in any organisation; Joan, the sexy secretary, and then the others. When establishing characters I like turning them on their heads a little to introduce unexpected traits. My favourite example of this appeared in the second series when Seamus Finnegan, the Irish labourer, appeared. Reggie took him to be thick like the traditional Irish jokes, and was shocked upon discovering he was a genius in administration!'

There is no question that *The Fall and Rise of Reginald Perrin* was very unusual and extremely funny. So brilliant was the creation that every character, every line of dialogue and every scene was a masterpiece, as were all the quirky features including the famous hippo representing Reggie's mother-in-law - yet another of David's fascinating inventions. 'I've certainly never had a mother-in-law remotely like a hippopotamus,' he laughs, 'but it's taking the old mother-in-law joke and making something new out of it that isn't offensive or particularly sexist.'

In September 1976, episode one of the first series, which as a pilot had been strong enough for the BBC chiefs to commission a whole seven-part series, was screened with Leonard playing the lead. But the actor was not David Nobbs's first choice.

The first offer to film a TV adaptation of his novel came from Granada TV, for whom David had just written a play. 'They were interested in screening Reggie Perrin as three 90-minute shows with Ronnie Barker as Reggie. When you consider I described the character as a big man with round shoulders, he seemed an ideal candidate.

'When I mentioned the offer to my agent, he advised against accepting it for two reasons. First, he didn't think it would give me enough exposure on mainstream TV, and, secondly, thought it would make a wonderful sitcom and knew the BBC were interested.'

An appointment was set up with Jimmy Gilbert, then Head of Comedy at the BBC. He was not slow in telling David how much he had loved his novel and was convinced it had the makings of a successful TV series. Gilbert then asked who David had in mind to play Reggie.

'I said Ronnie Barker, to which he

John Barron as C.J.

smiled and replied: "Fine! Leonard Rossiter it is then." I later found out the reason he didn't consider Ronnie was because he was already tied up with *Porridge, The Two Ronnies* and *Open All Hours.* His career was clearly mapped out whereas Leonard Rossiter – who had just started *Rising Damp* for ITV – was a key target for Jimmy, who wanted him for a BBC project. He saw this as an ideal vehicle with which to tempt Leonard.

After Leonard Rossiter had been signed up to play the lead, David Nobbs met the actor for the first time at the bar at Yorkshire TV, where Leonard was filming *Rising Damp.* 'The first thing he said to me was: "I'm really looking forward to doing your book; I think it's the second best comic novel by an English writer I've read recently." I thanked him for his kind words.

'Later he said to me: "I was very disappointed in you because when I said your book was the second best, you were supposed to be annoyed with me!" I didn't respond, but then asked what he thought was the best book, and he told me *A Touch of Daniel* by Peter Tinniswood, a friend of mine from my days on the *Sheffield Star.* But Len was disappointed by my response because he'd deliberately set out to upset me - which, in a way, was typical of the man because he was always testing people out.'

Today, it is hard to imagine anyone other than Leonard Rossiter playing Reggie Perrin, but Ronnie Barker would have relished the opportunity.

At the time, David Nobbs was disappointed the part was offered to Rossiter, but soon realised he was a perfect choice. 'Leonard could express the anxieties Reggie was experiencing in every move, expression and word he uttered. He could also combine pace with subtlety, which is very difficult. Most actors who try being

RONNIE BARKER   5/12/95

Dear Mr Webber.

What a funny series! What a funny writer! I wish I'd played Reggie - although, on second thought, if I had, the public would have been denied the brilliant, hilarious performance by Leonard Rositer. It was simply Perfect viewing.

Ronnie Barker

Gareth Gwenlan and Leonard Rossiter

subtle come across as slow, but not Leonard: he could rattle the lines out at a rate of knots while still retaining that degree of delicacy.

Although the pilot episode was produced by John Howard Davies, Gareth Gwenlan was also assigned to the project to prepare him for taking over the helm from episode two. *The Fall and Rise of Reginald Perrin* was Gareth's first major series for BBC1. 'I was quite an inexperienced TV producer, having worked mainly in the theatre. I'd done stuff for BBC2 but not really BBC1. John Howard Davies showed me the scripts and said that although he was doing the pilot he couldn't do the series because of an impending promotion to head of department and wanted to put my name forward for producing the series if commissioned.

'Jimmy Gilbert was understandably a little worried because I was only in my early 30s and the most junior producer in his department. But luckily he accepted John's recommendation, although it was with trepidation.'

Gareth - who went on to produce series two and three - believes the combination of good scripts and a strong cast was one of the main reasons the series was so successful. 'When you get scripts of the calibre David wrote and have the immensity of acting talent this country boasts, you could probably have got four or five first-rate actors for any of the parts and the series would still have worked. It's when you're struggling with less than perfect scripts that you have problems with casting.

Reginald Perrin

Pauline Yates

'But the Reggie Perrin cast was excellent. Although many of the actors for the primary characters were recruited by John, I couldn't fault his selections - they were perfect for their parts.

'Len was ideal for playing Reggie and John Barron, a versatile character actor who's always busy, was wonderful as C.J. Pauline Yates had a difficult role playing alongside Leonard. But she's unflappable and didn't let Len get to her, playing her part with absolute consistency. She's so dependable and a true professional. Sally-Jane Spencer was perfectly cast as Linda, the suburban bimbo, while Tim Preece, playing Tom, established a level of pomposity and intensity that was just right

John Barron

for his character. John Horsley played Doc Morrisey splendidly with a degree of vagueness that one will always associate with the character; some of it was deliberate vagueness but the rest was true Horsley - the part was made for him.

'Sue Nicholls was marvellous as Joan, Reggie's faithful secretary, while Trevor Adams and Bruce Bould – both very underrated actors – were perfectly cast as the yes-men David Harris-Jones and Tony Webster. Theresa Watson stepped in for the third series as David's wife, Prue, and played her part beautifully. Then, of course, there was Jimmy, played by Geoffrey Palmer. He's a wonderful actor and portrayed his character brilliantly.'

When the first series hit the screens, David - who wrote the scripts for all three series - was a little apprehensive about how well the programme had been received by the public. Not only was there a dearth of feedback from the BBC but he knew ITV were transmitting strong programmes that could potentially dent any chance Reggie Perrin had of attracting and sustaining a big audience. But frets were quickly dispelled upon visiting the Dragonara Hotel, Leeds. David recalls: 'I was staying in the hotel while working for Yorkshire TV in Leeds. The reception desk was on the second floor and as I waited for the lift three businessmen arrived and pressed the lift button again. They waited for a while before one turned to his colleagues and said: "Oh, come on. I didn't get where I am today by hanging around waiting for lifts!", to which the other two replied: "Great!", "Super!", before heading for the stairs. I couldn't believe my ears: it suddenly struck home that the catchphrases were catching on which meant the series was making an impact.'

David was pleased with how the novel translated to the small screen, though he understands some people prefer the original novels. 'That's fine by me,' he says. 'A book is a more complex product because it contains subplots, narrative and author's comments, which you can never match to the same degree of detail on the screen. And you invariably have to simplify some character complexities that can be developed in a book. However, adapting a novel for TV injects new qualities such as immediacy and a strength lacking on the pages of a novel. Overall, I was happy how it worked out.'

With the success of the first series it was not long before the BBC were discussing a further series with David Nobbs, as Gareth Gwenlan explains. 'Originally it was only ever

seen as one series because David's novel reached its own natural conclusion. But halfway through filming things were going

Sue Nicholls

so well that I asked David whether there was any chance of another series.'

He went away and thought long and hard about the matter and to Gareth's delight returned with a positive response. So Reggie, his family, boss and workmates were brought back for a second series, also a great success, and subsequently a third. And now the Perrin legacy is brought into the nineties with a fourth series.

Nowadays the success of any new TV series is helped along by exploiting attractive locations, but when the pilot episode for Reggie Perrin was filmed back in 1976, the production crew found themselves not being sent off to scenes of rolling countryside; they did not have to travel much further than a long stone's throw from Television Centre. Reggie's suburban home was found in a cul-de-sac off west London's Hanger Lane, while the Sunshine Desserts building was in the middle of a trading estate near the Old Oak Common Road in London. However, once the first series was commissioned location shooting did extend to five days at Longleat, Wiltshire, for the memorable episode two, set in the wildlife park; Witney, Oxfordshire, for some fantasy shots, and nearby Burford for the scene in episode five where C.J.'s fishing competition is ruined by loganberry juice turning the river red; and Dorset for the opening titles, faked suicide scene on the beach and most of episode six where Reggie roams the countryside under various guises.

The second series – which contained little location work – included Reggie opening his first Grot shop, which was in High Wycombe, while the Grot office block was sited off London's North Circular. The Grot logo which appeared on the building was created by shooting the office block through a glass plate with the logo painted on it.

Location filming for the third series in 1978 took place in Cheltenham because John B Hobbs, production manager on all three series, had experience of using the town in *Butterflies* with Gareth Gwenlan.

The popularity of the three series is irrefutable, and it swiftly attracted a loyal band of followers who stayed with the show throughout its screen life. In series one, the most watched episode was the penultimate with an audience figure of 8.5 million. For series two, the final episode attracted 10.5 million, and series three saw the third episode as the most popular with a rating of 10.2 million. But as producer Gareth Gwenlan explains, if one compared a programme's success purely on viewing figures, *The Fall and Rise of Reginald Perrin* would not have topped the charts.

'In a sense Reggie Perrin was one of those extraordinary series that wasn't a major success in audience terms, especially when you compare it with *To the Manor Born* – which I produced – that attracted audiences of up to 27 million, and never less than 18 million!

'Surprisingly, Reggie Perrin never won a single award and yet it was - and still is - regarded by many as an important work of comedy,' says Gareth. 'It was a big success in that it received wonderful write-ups, and attracted a sufficient audience to justify three series.'

Whereas many of these equally popular programmes have slipped into obscurity and have not even received an airing on the satellite channel UK Gold, *The Fall and Rise of Reginald Perrin* remains as fresh and energetic today as it did on first screening, with recent repeats still commanding impressive audiences and consistently appearing in UK Gold's Top Ten programmes.

So why has the programme become such a cult show? Among the many reasons why Reggie Perrin has earned the accolade of

being regarded as a 'classic' in the history of the small screen is undoubtedly the quantity and quality of the comic lines packed into each 30-minute episode, something David Nobbs always tries to achieve in his comedy work. 'Occasionally I teach on writing courses and something I always stress to students is that for a comedy to be successful, every scene and every character must be funny - and that's what I set out to achieve in Reggie.

'If you've only got one funny character and all the others simply serving that person then things rapidly tire. I've been told that Reggie Perrin advanced the comedy genre because before most sitcoms had no narrative: the TV company could transmit episodes in any order and it wouldn't have mattered – that's not the case now.

'Inevitably, this development would have taken place at some point; I just like to think that, perhaps, Reggie Perrin caused it to happen a little quicker.'

From David Nobbs's point of view, the second series was the funniest and most inventive. 'The first was the heart of the matter; it was the dilemma that kicked off the extreme actions Reggie was to take.

'The second saw the series hit its peak in respect of invention: I wanted Reggie to be successful in something he viewed as his protest – in this case, the objection of companies selling rubbish under false pretences. Of course, his absurd idea soon became successful but embarrassing to Reggie who set out to destroy Grot but to no avail.'

Gareth Gwenlan believes the second series set such a high standard it was almost impossible for the third series to match it. 'It was unquestionably the best of the three, and in my view will only be surpassed, I hope, by the fourth which I think will be excellent!'

In both the producer's and writer's eyes the third series – although still popular with viewers – was not as strong as its predecessors. 'The Grot series was such a superb, zany idea David and I were unsure how we could ever top it. While there were elements of series three that were wonderfully clever, it didn't hit the target quite as often as number two.'

David feels the commune idea worked better in the novel. 'The concept of all the people visiting the community was easier to develop in the book because I had more time to describe them. On TV, many of the visitors turned into caricatures because time constraints meant we had to skate over them. Also, introducing so many characters meant there were a lot of people taking the comic impetus off the main characters, and the whole series at times came across as a compilation of sketches.'

Another plus point for all three series was the crisp production and scarcity of mistakes which made for a highly professional, well-executed collection of episodes. Gareth Gwenlan feels there were several reasons why filming went so smoothly, including the influence of Leonard, who in many respects was the driving force behind the show.

'Len inspired confidence and didn't suffer fools gladly. Anyone working on the production knew they had to try to run as fast as he could, which took some doing. The pace of each episode was so quick and was conducive to generating a highly professional atmosphere.

'With Leonard it was a case of everyone giving their utmost in everything they did. He always did and expected the same level of commitment from others.'

The appeal of Reggie Perrin extends beyond the British Isles to Australia, New Zealand, Canada, many parts of Europe and particularly the USA, where it was successful enough to spawn an American version called *Reggie,* starring *Soap*'s Richard Mulligan. As far as David Nobbs was concerned, the American equivalent missed the point. 'I didn't like it. They changed too much and failed to do their spadework regarding understanding the routine of the life from which Reggie was rebelling. This routine had to be established at the start so that people could understand why he was like he was. The Americans didn't do this which meant there was no tension. They even made C.J. out to be a young whizz-kid which was all wrong.'

But the original episodes have always been popular in the States and continue to be shown on Public Service Broadcasting throughout the country. The Americans' awareness of the series was proven a few months ago when David got chatting to an American teacher who was visiting England.

'I was in the bar of London's Norfolk Hotel one afternoon. There was only one other person there and we got talking and he told me he taught English and was touring the country.

'He'd visited Oxford but hadn't got to Cambridge yet. I told him it was lovely there and he must try to visit before he headed home. He said he would try because he'd written an article for the Cambridge University Press on TV adaptations of Joseph Conrad's work. I told him I found that interesting because I too did adaptations.

'We carried on talking and at the end of our conversation he asked my name. When I told him, he said: "Nobbs? Bit of a cock-up on the catering front?" I was really chuffed an American knew the phrase.'

David Nobbs

THE CREATOR

As David Nobbs's parents and grandparents were all teachers, one could easily have assumed that he would follow in their footsteps – but the thought never crossed his mind.

'The strange thing was they all taught maths!' says David. 'My standard of maths was good enough to keep score during darts matches, but that was all; so I never had plans of keeping the family tradition alive.'

Born in Orpington, Kent, in 1935, David – an only child – was evacuated to Marlborough during the war at the age of four. While living in Wiltshire, he began his education at a local school, before returning to Orpington and a close encounter with a German bomb.

'We went back home just before the flying bombs began which was a big mistake because the very last doodlebug to fall during the war fell in Orpington, bringing my bedroom ceiling crashing down. I was in the room at the time but luckily unhurt.'

David continued his education at Bickley Hall, a prep school that is now defunct, until his father sent him at 13 to Marlborough College, where he stayed five years. 'It was at Marlborough that I started writing. I wrote a few articles for the college magazine; the first one published was my review of the cadet corp 'Day of Action' in Savernake Forest which was a humorous review. I remember it contained the line: "As we marched down Marlborough High Street regarded by some good judges as the widest high street in Marlborough . . . ", which must have been my first published joke.'

At 18, David completed the obligatory two years national service in the Royal Corps of Signals. During this time he undertook a correspondence course in journalism which put him in good stead for studying at Cambridge – which he did upon returning to civvy street.

'I read Classics at St John's College and for the first two years discovered I'd lost my real impetus for learning, so I turned to writing for the university paper and sketches for the Footlights.

'Later I discovered Peter Cook had read my articles at Cambridge and had loved them, which was very flattering.'

After graduating, David's first job was with the *Sheffield Star*, but his journalistic career got off to an unfortunate start. 'It began with a misprint!' he smiles. 'My first article for the paper was reporting a break in, but the very first word was misprinted, and read: "Thives broke into the home of Miss Emily Braithwaite."

'I had a few other misprints while working on the paper including a gloriously meaningless paragraph under the heading: "Sinatra Gardner". It was a one paragraph column filler stating: "The on-off, on-off engagement of Frank Sinatra and Ava Gardner was today authoritatively stated to be oww." It was meaningless because no one knew whether it was on or off.'

In 1960 – after two years with the paper – David headed for London, renting a small bedsit in West Hampstead. He continued with his writing but without any luck. During this period he wrote ten stage plays that were never performed, and a novel he started while working in Sheffield remained incomplete. David was at a low ebb. 'To make matters worse I was also trying to get over a failed romance – it was a depressing period of my life.'

Lack of money forced David into taking a job as a voucher clerk in an advertising agency. The boredom of his working day was tolerated only by the thought that he could return to his writing in the evenings – but he was struggling to summon up enough energy and motivation even to pick up a pen.

But his luck was shortly to change. He returned to journalism with a job on the weekly *St Pancras Chronicle*, where his responsibilities involved very little work. 'All I seemed to do was attend endless council meetings.'

While he was working on the paper a new TV programme was screened. The humour of *That Was the Week That Was* – which ran between 1962-63 – struck a chord with

Leonard Rossiter and David Nobbs

David who decided to have a go at writing a sketch. Once completed, he phoned the production office. 'A girl asked me to post it to her but when I explained it was topical and would be old news by the time she received it, she asked me to hang on. Then David Frost – who recognised my name from the Cambridge articles – came on the line and told me he'd send a taxi to collect it.'

When David Nobbs phoned a couple of days later he could not believe it when David Frost classed the sketch as 'super!' and wanted to use it. 'It was wonderful news. After telling everybody I felt rather embarrassed when only one line was used – but at least it was a start.'

The following week they used a whole sketch of David's, and in no time at all he had given up his job in journalism to write full-time. 'Luckily, the struggle was over,' he says. 'Until then I hadn't any idea where my writing career

Leonard Rossiter and David Nobbs on a visit to the Arts Council Shop to sign David's book *The Better World of Reginald Perrin*

was heading. Those years had been very difficult: I had little money and was depressed much of the time.'

David became a regular writer for *That Was the Week That Was* and quickly progressed to other projects, including *Lance at Large*, which he wrote with Peter Tinniswood for comedian Lance Percival. Unfortunately, the show did not work. 'The series was very misconceived although Peter and I didn't realise it at the time. The producer wanted Lance to work without the help of any other regular characters. That works with a genius,' says David, 'such as someone in the Chaplin mould, but it didn't with Lance. He's a very good actor but the show did him no favours at all. It was entirely the wrong way to go about it and we were too inexperienced to realise.'

The experience set David back slightly, but he soon recovered his confidence and continued writing. Two novels quickly followed: *Ostrich Country* and *A Piece of the Sky is Missing*, and he began writing for some of the nation's top comedians such as: Frankie Howerd, Dick Emery, Tommy Cooper, Ken Dodd, Jimmy Tarbuck and Les Dawson – including *68 Sez Les* for Yorkshire TV. David Nobbs was beginning to establish himself as one of the country's finest comic writers and when in 1975 his novel *The Death of Reginald Perrin* (later reissued as *The Fall and Rise of Reginald Perrin*) hit the bookshelves, the author had reached the big time.

The success of the Reggie Perrin novels and the TV adaptations meant David was now in a strong enough position financially to choose what projects he worked on, including writing two series of *Fairly Secret Army,* starring Geoffrey Palmer as Major Harry Truscott, a right-wing fanatic who formed his own private army – a character closely resembling Jimmy in Reggie Perrin.

'The second series worked better than the first. I started off by not writing enough storylines and there wasn't enough going on. I relied too heavily on people loving the character as much as I did – and that's always a dreadful mistake, as I found out.

Other series including: *The Life and Times of Henry Pratt, Rich Tea and Sympathy* and *A Bit of a Do* – which was adapted from his novels – brought more success.

Written for Yorkshire TV, *A Bit of a Do* was screened in 1989 and highlighted the social rivalry between two families. The idea for the original novel was sparked off by David's casual observations of life.

'I lived in Herefordshire at the time and kept being invited to various functions, including two dentists' dinner dances; an angling Christmas party and a charity horse-racing evening. The funny thing was that I kept meeting the same people at all these dos and realised that here was a fascinating idea for a TV series or a book – or both, as it turned out.'

Throughout his writing career David has used everyday life to influence his ideas and his writing. He is particularly interested in people's occupations. 'I'm currently writing a series for BBC Drama about a formation dance team called Cheek to *Cheek*. I had great fun working out all the dancers' occupations, and have finally ended up with a tattooist, a dry cleaner, a dentist and a chef at a Happy Eater, just to mention a few.

'A series set in a dentist's surgery or a dry cleaners would have very limited fun because not enough interesting things would happen, but a series, for example, about a dry cleaner in a dance team always talking about his dry cleaning problems and how misunderstood he is strikes me as hilarious,' says David.

During his successful career, David Nobbs – who lives in North Yorkshire – has written 12 novels and a myriad of TV scripts.

Leonard Rossiter

'With a false nose that isn't and a mouth like the grin on a Halloween pumpkin, his face by itself is a piece of theatre,' was how one journalist described Leonard Rossiter. The words paint a rather exaggerated picture of the man, but there is no doubting his physical features were very distinctive as was his inimitable style of acting. And it was these qualities which propelled the actor to the top of his profession and are sorely missed today – 12 years after his untimely death.

Every now and again the entertainment world is blessed by the emergence of a talent that flourishes into greatness. Sadly, this occurrence is rare but when such an actor appears on the scene you soon know it, and Rossiter was one of the industry's elite.

Born in Liverpool in 1926, the son of John and Elizabeth Rossiter, Leonard was educated at Collegiate Grammar School. He excelled in languages and wanted to become a teacher – ambitions that were tapped during his national service. Rising to the rank of sergeant, he taught illiterate soldiers to read and write while based in Germany with the Army Education Corps.

After demob, Leonard, who spoke French and German fluently, saw his plans of studying languages at Liverpool University thwarted when his father – a voluntary ambulanceman during the war – was killed during an air raid in 1942.

With his mother to support, Leonard discarded ideas of an academic career and joined the Commercial Union Insurance Company in 1948, earning £210 per annum as a clerk in the claims and accidents department.

It was during the six years spent in insurance that Leonard had his first taste of acting. 'Len always told the story about the evening he was picking a girlfriend up from the local amateur dramatics company,' says his widow, actress Gillian Raine. 'He sat at the back of the hall and watched, but wasn't at all impressed. When she asked him what he thought of the performance, he told her he could do better. She suggested he tried, so he did – and that was how his acting career began.'

An insurance clerk by day and a callow thespian by night, Leonard became the first of the Rossiter family to tread the boards when he joined a local acting company. His brother, John, was a scientist who helped design the Thames flood barrier, while his father had been a barber. 'But he was also a bookie at a time when gambling was still illegal,' explains Gillian. 'While customers had their hair cut, at the same time they could lay bets because he also ran a secret bookmakers. He got to know many of the variety actors working in the city, and even played golf with George Formby's father.'

Leonard's stage debut was in Rattigan's *Flare Path*, with the Adastra Players. A local critic reported that he had an inclination to speak his lines too quickly – something he was wise enough never to change and which has since become one of the hallmarks of his fine acting style. His incredible pace of delivery was something Gillian noticed when they first worked together in *Semi-Detached* at Coventry's Belgrade Theatre in the autumn of '63.

'I remember saying to myself: "Oh God, how are we going to get this across to the audience because no one will ever hear what he says because he talks too fast. But, of course, the audience did and they found him just as funny as I did.'

It was this speed of delivery that resulted in David Nobbs having to write slightly more script than one would expect for 30-minute episodes. 'His delivery was extremely fast and other people took their cue from him, so I ended up writing what would have been 35 minutes on any other production.

'While we were rehearsing one episode we suddenly realised we only had 28 minutes of script. Len said this would be extended to 29 minutes 30 seconds with all the laughs, so we didn't worry any more about it. When we recorded it in front of the audience, he speeded up even more and we finished on 27 minutes!'

When Gillian Raine began working with Leonard it did not take her long to realise he had a bright future as an actor. 'It is impossible to say that someone is going to become successful because there is always a certain amount of luck involved in this business. But it was obvious Len had great talent and, given the right opportunities, would do well as an actor.'

Leonard's amateur days were becoming increasingly busy as he began working with more than one amateur society at a time. It was soon apparent that he had reached an important crossroads in his life: if he wanted to further his acting career he had

Leonard Rossiter appearing in *Semi-Detached* with Gillian Raine (centre) and Joan Sanderson (right)

to turn professional which meant ditching his job as an insurance clerk. At the age of 27, he did just that.

Swapping the stability and security of a regular income for the jobbing actor's precarious lifestyle was an enormous step. But he never let the pressures associated with the decision affect him: as far as Leonard was concerned acting was his future; it was also far more appealing than living out his life in the boredom of an insurance office.

His professional career began at Preston Rep. playing Bert Gay in *The Gay Dog*. Two other members of the cast were John Barron and Frederick Jaeger, who also made an appearance in Reggie Perrin. 'Len was dedicated and a perfectionist even in those days,' says Frederick.

'He was so intense about his work which meant he wasn't the most relaxed of people. But he was always word perfect and one of the most professional actors I've ever worked with. He expected everyone to work as hard as he did. You had to keep up with him, otherwise you'd know it!'

Upon leaving Preston, spells followed at Wolverhampton and Salisbury before he joined the Bristol Old Vic Company at the city's Theatre Royal. Leonard felt the two seasons spent at Bristol were crucial because they established a solid base from which his career could bloom.

Acting in the same company was Peter Bowles who remembers a terrible row with Leonard. 'We were a double act in a panto called *Hooray for Daisy!* It got a bit tricky because my comedy timing was different from his; when it came to choosing a style that was right for our roles we couldn't agree and ended up having a tremendous argument. Even so, I enjoyed working with Len and we developed a great respect for each other.'

Years later, Peter worked with Leonard in an episode of the classic comedy *Rising*

Leonard Rossiter as Rigsby in *Rising Damp*

Damp. 'When I arrived at the studios I sensed immediately that everyone seemed very nervous of him. They kept warning me not to upset him because he was very particular.

'I'd always got on well with Len and by now we were old friends. When filming began I started making suggestions about how scenes could be improved. Everybody

seemed to duck for cover but, as I expected, he listened and we tried out my ideas.

'I could never understand why everyone was so nervous of him because if you put forward a good idea that was worth trying he would never dismiss it.

'Len was a remarkable actor with a unique style. I remember his spring-footedness more than anything. It was as if he had springs in his shoes. His stylistic approach was very powerful and was something he was unaware of until later in his career, when he began exploiting it. He was a great actor.'

By the mid 60s, Leonard had experienced working in all strands of the entertainment world. His film appearances included Whymper in *A Kind of Loving*; Phillips in *The Sporting Life* and Shadrack in *Billy Liar*.

On the small screen he had already appeared in numerous productions such as *The Avengers* and *Z Cars*, playing the derisive Detective-Inspector Bamber.

Whatever medium he worked in during his career, the love for his favoured medium – theatre – never waned, as Gillian explains.

'Many people remember Leonard solely for his TV work, yet he did more stage work than anything else. Between TV projects he always returned to the theatre, and got slightly annoyed whenever he was referred to as a small screen actor.'

Gillian holds nothing but happy memories

years later, that we married.'

Within that period Leonard's career progressed well. Although he was not offered the lead when *Semi-Detached* moved to the West End, he did have the opportunity of taking the play to Broadway – though he probably wished he had not. After two weeks of well-received previews the critics turned against the

show when it opened on Broadway. Within a week it had closed.

of the days spent working with Leonard at Coventry in *Semi-Detached*. 'I can remember we laughed all the time. The play was well written and very funny, but being a new production we had the chance to shape it the way we felt best and Leonard's influence was crucial to this process.'

Gradually their friendship developed. 'He was married to Josephine Tewson at the time but their marriage was in trouble. Although we decided to live together soon after we met, it wasn't until 1972, eleven

In 1969, Leonard's brilliant virtuoso performance as Hitler in Brecht's *The Resistible Rise of Arturo Ui*, made him a West End star. In the audience one evening during the play's successful run was Richard Briers, who was impressed by Rossiter's performance.

'His energy in the part was extraordinary. He was one of the great eccentric actors and certainly a one-off.'

His occasional excursion onto the big screen continued and his TV career was just as busy, but it was not until 1974 and the advent of *Rising Damp* followed quickly by *The Fall and Rise of Reginald Perrin,* that Leonard became a household name.

When Reggie Perrin was being cast, BBC producer Gareth Gwenlan visited Leonard at his home to discuss the part. 'I was

Leonard Rossiter raises a glass to Joan Collins

shown upstairs to his office, next to his wine cellar, which was at the top of the house!' says Gareth. 'Without making it obvious, he began probing me intensely on my knowledge of David Nobbs's book.

'When we started filming series one, each day was like the first day at school. With his usual quiet humour Leonard was always testing me. I had to make sure I'd done just as much homework as he had because if I hadn't he would soon find out – it was a matter of respect.

'It was a huge learning curve for me but a valuable one: I learnt more about comedy, directing comedy and comedy performance from him in three months than I had in the previous ten years in TV.'

Other TV roles followed but nothing seemed to live up to the high standards set by the two vintage comedies *Rising Damp* and *The Fall and Rise of Reginald Perrin,* but he did attract a fresh audience with a series of successful Cinzano adverts with Joan Collins.

There is no doubting Leonard was a perfectionist. He worked incredibly hard to make the most of whatever he was working on and expected the same degree of dedication from fellow thespians. Occasionally people viewed him as difficult to work with and felt he did not suffer fools gladly. 'Len would not go along with things that he wasn't happy with and had the confidence to say something about it rather than put up with it. Because of this frankness some people felt he was difficult,' says Gillian.

'What people sometimes forgot was that playing the lead in many of the productions meant he carried a great amount of responsibility on his shoulders. If something wasn't of the highest possible standard it would reflect badly on him.'

Away from the spotlight, Leonard was a

private man who enjoyed a variety of sports and was a connoisseur of wine. 'He was always energetic,' Gillian remembers. 'If we went on holiday we had to go somewhere that had squash courts. He wasn't the sort of person to sit on a beach. If we did, it wouldn't be long before he was up running along the beach.'

Leonard's career and life came to a shocking end while he was appearing in Joe Orton's *Loot* at London's Lyric Theatre in 1984.

Appearing with Leonard in the play, ironically about death, was actor David John. He will never forget that tragic evening. 'The day before he had told me he wasn't feeling very well because he had chest pains and planned seeing the doctor.

'The following evening I asked how he had got on at the doctor's and he said: "Fine. He gave me a check over and I'm as fit as a fiddle." That was that and we continued with the play.

'I was sitting in my dressing room when a call went out reminding Len that his entrance was coming up. I couldn't believe it because he was never late for one of his scenes. Then when I heard over the tannoy the actors on stage improvising because they had run out of lines after Len had missed his entrance, I knew something was terribly wrong.'

David rushed to Leonard's dressing room, pushed the door open and found him slumped in an armchair. 'The first thing I noticed was his grey complexion. Initially, I was so shocked I didn't know what to do but within seconds other members of the cast arrived. Gemma Craven felt his pulse and said he was dead. I couldn't believe it and tried giving him the kiss of life and massaging his heart.

'I just could not imagine that he was dead, but I was wrong. When the ambulancemen arrived I still thought there was a chance he would be OK, especially when they put an oxygen mask over his mouth. But when I saw two of the doctors who had been in the audience shake their heads to each other as he was carried from the dressing room, I knew there was no chance.

'The rest of the evening was a blur as we finished the performance. The play

Leonard Rossiter as he appeared in *Loot*

continued for a further three months before it finally closed.'

Leonard had died of a disease of the heart muscles, a congenital defect that could have struck at any time. That evening the world lost one of its finest actors and his talents are still sadly missed.

SERIES ONE:

'Sunshine Desserts-Escaping the Rat Race'

EPISODE ONE:

"Eleven minutes late, signal failure at Vauxhall." (Reggie)

"I didn't get where I am today by selling ice cream tasting of bookends, pumice stone and West Germany!" (C.J.)

As Reggie prepares for yet another day of his uneventful life, the frustrations and irritations begin to surface, including losing patience with wife, Elizabeth, during their little morning ritual:

ELIZABETH: Umbrella.
REGGIE: Thank you, darling.
ELIZABETH: Briefcase.
REGGIE: Thank you, darling.
ELIZABETH: Back at the normal time?
REGGIE: Of course.
ELIZABETH: Have a good day at the office.
REGGIE: I won't.

After leaving home for the monotonous trudge to Sunshine Desserts via Coleridge

Reggie leaves for the office . . .

Avenue, Tennyson Avenue, Wordsworth Drive and train from Norbiton - which is constantly 11 minutes late - he suddenly imagines his mother-in-law as a hippo - an image that remained with him throughout his life.

On the train, nose-blowing neighbour Peter Cartwright infuriates Reggie: not only does he constantly finish the crossword first, but he is always hankieless and scrounging various makeshift alternatives, including Reggie's Venezuelan trade supplement. Once used, Peter pushes the bundle of snot-ridden newspaper under the seat.

This episode exposes the routines, predictabilities and expectations affecting the eponymous sales executive's life. It also reveals the deep rut in which he finds himself embedded and from which he tries desperately to escape.

Even his arrival at Sunshine Desserts triggers off another tired routine that Reggie's been tolerating for 25 years. After narrowly missing being clobbered on the head when one of the company's nameplate

. . . and boards the train

letters above the doorway tumbles to the floor, he enters his office at the usual time: 11 minutes late; is met by Joan, his devoted secretary; throws his umbrella unsuccessfully at the hat stand and settles down for another day's slog.

While dictating letters the phone rings: C.J. wants to plan a meeting. Reggie

Ray Marioni

Character: Waiter.
Series 1, Episode 1.
Born: London.
Credits include: TV – Coronation Street, Grange Hill, Auf Wiedersehen, Pet.
Film – Loser Takes All.
Update: Until recently owned a secondhand shop in London's Harrow Road. Was often cast as a waiter.

Norman Mitchell

Character: Ron Napier who represented Transport Dept, Sunshine Desserts at ice cream tasting.
Series 1, Episode 1.
Born: Sheffield.
Training: Medicine at Sheffied University.
Early career: Nine years in army.
Credits include: TV – All Creatures Great and Small, Yes Minister.
Film – Barry Lyndon, Revenge of the Pink Panther.
P.S. Made over 2,000 TV and 100 movie appearances.

33

Reggie consults Doc Morrisey

suggests any time that morning, C.J. opts for 4 p.m. – a stiff reminder to Reggie of the supposed powers afforded to him by his seniority.

During the meeting – which is also attended by the fawning Tony and David ('Great!' and 'Super!', respectively) – Reggie announces an ice cream tasting in his office on Wednesday to help launch the exotic ices project.

The following day (Wednesday) Reggie arrives late as usual, but when he begins fantasising about Joan he decides it is time to visit the firm's doctor, Doc Morrisey, which – as expected – is a complete waste of time.

DOC: Had any dreams about naked sportswomen?
REGGIE: Yes! As a matter of fact I have. How on earth did you know? Only last night I was watching the Whiteman Cup at Wimbledon. Everyone was stark naked – even the line judges!
DOC: Who won?
REGGIE: To be honest, I didn't bother much with the scores; I think it was the one with the . . . very big first serves.
DOC: I say, your ticker's racing like the clappers – not surprising, really. Do you find you can't finish the crossword like you used to; nasty taste in the mouth in the mornings; can't stop thinking about sex; can't start doing anything about sex; wake up with a sweat in the morning; keep falling asleep during Play for Today?
REGGIE: Extraordinary, that's exactly how I've been feeling, yes.
DOC: So do I, wonder what it is?
(The Doc gives Reggie the old faithful: two aspirin)

The ice cream tasting is a fiasco. Not only do Reggie and David Harris-Jones feel sick after eating too many ice creams, but the computer fouls up the results and lists bookends, pumice stone and West Germany as the favourite varieties. Reggie goes home fed up.

By Thursday, Reggie is close to breaking point, though he must wait another four episodes before doing anything about it. He lags behind with breakfast and is acerbic towards Elizabeth's concerns with minutiae, including a piece of yellow fluff on his suit. Today, he decides to do everything differently.

Ignoring the fact that he has an early morning meeting scheduled, Reggie catches a later train, allowing him time to enjoy the clement weather. Seasonal manpower shortages at Clapham Junction result in

Roland MacLeod

Character: Morris Coates, ad executive employed by Sunshine Desserts and Grot.
Series 1, Episode 1.
Series 2, Episode 4.
Early career: Considered becoming a clergyman.
Born: London.
Credits include: TV – *Please Sir!*, *The Fenn Street Gang.*
Film – *A Fish Called Wanda*, *Le Petomane* (with Leonard Rossiter).
P.S. Frequently cast as clergyman.

the later train also being 11 minutes late. When Reggie finally arrives, Tony Webster, Morris Coates and Esther Pigeon are already waiting to discuss advertising for the exotic ices project.

After a brief discussion the meeting is brought to an abrupt end when Reggie admits he cannot be bothered with it all because life is too short.

Reggie refuses Tony's invite for the customary Thursday lunchtime drink and opts for something different: a balanced three-course meal of ravioli, followed by ravioli, followed by ravioli, at an Italian restaurant.

Suffering the after effects of stuffing himself with pasta, Reggie spends the entire afternoon bloated and unable to move. But he can just concentrate enough to dictate a letter to the Traffic Manager B.R. (Southern Region).

> *Dear Sir,*
> *Every morning my train is 11 minutes late. This is infuriating. This morning I took a later train: this was also 11 minutes late. This also is infuriating. Why don't you retime all your trains to arrive 11 minutes late and then they'll all be on time?*
> *Yours faithfully,*
> *Reginald Iolanthe Perrin*

Back at home, Reggie explains to Elizabeth that the reason he calls her mother a hippopotamus is because he is fed up with doing things the same all the time. Elizabeth, sensing her husband's troubles, stresses her love for him, before telling Reggie dinner consists of ravioli followed by ice cream.

'I REMEMBER the opening titles of a man swimming out to sea were filmed during the summer of '76 on a Dorset beach.

Jacki Piper

Character: Esther Pigeon, market research expert.
Series 1, Episode 1.
Series 2, Episode 4.
Born: Birmingham.
Training: Birmingham Theatre School.
Credits include: TV – *The Two Ronnies, The Generation Game, Dick Emery, Call My Bluff, Dangerfield, The Bill.*
P.S. Familiar face from the Carry On films.

Leonard ran along the beach, stripped down to flesh-coloured trunks and headed for the sea. But as he disappeared from view down a dip, Ken Barker, a stuntman, took over.

'The beach was deserted but hadn't been 20 minutes earlier when Gareth Gwenlan instructed me to clear it of its 200 plus holidaymakers – and all within half an hour!

'At first, I thought it impossible, but succeeded by explaining to the people on the first cluster of deckchairs what was going on and asking them to pass it on. There may have been hundreds of people watching from the dunes, but the beach was deserted and I hadn't moved an inch!'
(John B. Hobbs)

Employees of Sunshine Desserts gather for the ice cream tasting

EPISODE TWO:

Reggie Perrin. 46, senior sales executive. Bored. Under stress. Has begun to behave oddly.

"Eleven minues late, defective junction box at New Malden." (Reggie)

"I didn't get where I am today by waffling!" (C.J.)

The stresses of life are taking their toll on Reggie, so Elizabeth persuades him to ask C.J. for four weeks holiday.

The following day (Friday) Reggie arrives at Sunshine Desserts 11 minutes late to be reminded by Joan of the mindless bureaucracy riddling the company, which is partly responsible for Reggie's despair.

JOAN: Colin Edmonds from Admin rang; it seems you have the wrong hat stand – yours has four pegs.
REGGIE: So?
JOAN: It seems you only have entitlement to a three-peg stand.
REGGIE: Oh my God! Is this the beginning of the end? Food firm executive found hanging naked from minute hand of Big Ben. 'I'm only a three-peg man!' he cried.

Joan reminds Reggie that David and Tony are due shortly to discuss the trial sales areas for the exotic ices project, which he has forgotten. Having also forgotten to allocate the regions his two subordinates will be responsible for, Reggie quickly decides by drawing round a waste paper basket and Joan's handbag. When Tony comments that 20% of his area is in the

sea, Reggie tells him about the trawlers, tankers, liners, dredgers, submarines and Isle of Man ferries that will help make up this whole new sales area.

Later, Reggie dictates a few letters, including one of his more unusual compositions to the manager of Get-it-Quick Supermarket, Get-it-Quick House, 77 Car Park Road, Birmingham.

Dear Sir,
Thank you for your comments of the 27th. Your complaints about late

Joan takes a letter

36

*delay are not only completely
unjustified, but also ungrammatical.
The fault lies in your inability to fill
out an order form correctly. You are
in effect a pompous, illiterate baboon.
Yours faithfully,
Reginald I. Perrin*

Finally, after summoning enough courage
to confront C.J. with his holiday request,
Reggie's nerves overwhelm him and instead
of four weeks, he ends up being granted
only half a day. He tries convincing himself

Terence Conoley

Character: Peter Cartwright, fellow
commuter of Reggie's.
Series 1, Episodes 1, 2, 4, 5.
Series 2, Episodes 2, 4.
Early career: Nine years in the army.
Born: Colchester.
Credits include: TV – Misleading
Cases, Fawlty Towers.
Film – Tiara Tahiti.
P.S. Only actor to make two guest
appearances on Fawlty Towers.

it is better than nothing until his
quiet afternoon is torn apart with
the arrival of Jimmy, who leaves
with a bundle of groceries after
yet another 'cock-up on the
catering front', and Linda who
asks whether Elizabeth and
Reggie will take her family to the
safari park tomorrow because
Tom has crashed their car.

Saturday is greeted with hot
sunshine, not the sort of weather
for driving around a safari park,
hermetically sealed within
Reggie's car, with Tom and Linda
stinking of last night's squid and
garlic, and their annoying kids,
Adam and Jocasta, contributing
to the eventful afternoon by doing
'biggies'.

Finally, after his car overheats,
Reggie loses not just his temper,
but his faculties as well, and
leaps from his car within the lion
reserve. But he quickly comes to
his senses when the lions begin
licking their lips and charging
towards him.

'I REMEMBER filming the episode at Longleat. It was the middle of a heatwave and temperatures reached 90 degrees. We wanted to show lots of cars parading around the safari park, not just Reggie's, but no other visitors turned up because it was too hot. So along with members of the production team I spent most of the day just driving round!'   **(David Nobbs)**

'I ordered three lions for the episode. One was mounted on a plinth which looked realistic once we put grass round its feet and tied a nylon wire to its tail which someone swished occasionally. Another was lying down and looked OK, but the third was simply a lion skin. I was wondering how I could use it when a prop boy said: "Don't worry. I'll get inside, wriggle around a bit and try looking like a lion." He looked too thin so we stuffed straw inside the skin as well and got ready to film. I looked at the other lions: one's tail was swishing, the other was lying down and I was just about to start filming when I noticed a wisp of cigarette smoke coming out of one of the lion's mouth: the prop boy was inside having a fag!

'After apologising, a hand came out of the lion but before he could put the cigarette out, he'd set the tinder dry grass alight – it was a nightmare.'

(Gareth Gwenlan)

Abigail Morgan & Robert Hillier

Characters: Jocasta and Adam, Tom and Linda's children. Series 1&2.

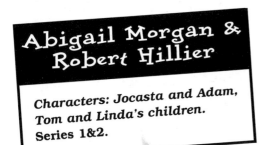

Penny Leatherbarrow

Character: Tea Lady.
Series 1, Episode 2.
Credits include: TV – *Coronation Street* (Cath Spinks), *Rosie*, *Angels*.
Update: Career still dominated by TV.

Tom, Jocasta, Adam, Linda, Reggie and Elizabeth on the family outing to Longleat

Pauline Yates

ELIZABETH PERRIN

Some people view Elizabeth Perrin as the long-suffering wife of a man never at ease with life. In reality, although she often – quite understandably – showed signs of frustration and annoyance with her husband's bizarre attitudes, she never desired anything other than to support and make her husband happy.

In hindsight, Elizabeth must have realised that dreams of living a 'normal life' were shattered the day she married Reggie Perrin. Although she led a highly complex existence, she made the most of what she had, ceremoniously enduring all of Reggie's harebrained schemes.

When her husband vanished – presumed dead after leaving his clothes on a Dorset beach – Elizabeth befriended Henry Possett. Shortly after announcing her engagement, she scrapped plans of marriage upon discovering the bearded Martin Wellbourne – who had suddenly appeared in her life – was Reggie in disguise.

Back with her true love, Elizabeth encouraged Reggie to reveal his real identity to friends and family, which ultimately led to his sacking from Sunshine Desserts. Money needs drove Elizabeth out to work as Tony Webster and David Harris Jones's secretary at the dessert giant, until she was also sacked for typing a memo about soggy trifle sponges that revealed too many truths.

When Reggie launched Grot, Elizabeth took charge of the company's expansion into Europe; but after her husband destroyed the empire he had created, they faked their own suicides and toured the countryside as Mr and Mrs Gossamer until boredom set in. The next project in their eventful lives was the commune, with Elizabeth as secretary.

For the fourth series, Elizabeth Perrin has reached her 70s and is a widow following Reggie's untimely death after being flattened by a falling billboard.

One of the fondest memories Pauline has of playing Elizabeth Perrin is receiving bundles of fan mail, usually from middle-aged men.

'They all wished they had a wife like Elizabeth,' smiles Pauline, who was amazed at how popular the show became. 'The scripts were good, but I've been in series before where scripts have been funny yet the programme's failed.

'But Reggie Perrin seemed to hit a chord with so many people – particularly older men who, perhaps, saw Reggie's situation as very close to their own. I'm pleased to be associated with it and it's one of my career highlights.'

When the BBC offered Pauline the role of Elizabeth she did not hesitate in accepting. 'Obviously I was pleased to be offered the work,' she says, 'but I was also attracted to the idea because I'd worked with Leonard before and knew that with him in the pilot it could only be a success.'

Playing Reggie's wife was inevitably a challenge, but that did not deter Pauline, who liked the character. 'Elizabeth was a kind of 'yes' woman, agreeing and supporting her husband. But, unknown to her, she was also part of Reggie's angst, even though she was happy going along with his bizarre ways.'

Pauline has enjoyed playing Elizabeth again in *The Legacy of Reginald Perrin*. 'It's been wonderful, especially meeting up with all the old faces once more. And, of course, David Nobbs's scripts are as meticulous as ever.'

Many critics question whether the void left behind by the death of Leonard Rossiter can be bridged, but Pauline is quietly confident. 'Only time will tell for certain whether it can grip viewers' imaginations like before,' she says, 'but the image of Reggie's so strong and the other characters are extremely funny, that I think the new series will be a success in its own right.'

Born in St Helens, Merseyside, Pauline knew from a young age that she wanted to be an actress, but never confided in anybody. 'There didn't seem much point because whenever I told anyone they shrieked and told me I couldn't!'

After leaving school (Childwall Valley High School) she secured a summer job at

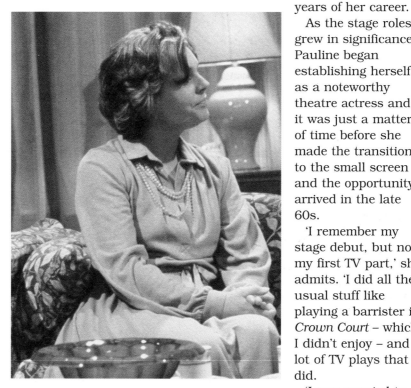

Oldham Rep. 'During the holiday I asked my mum whether I could work at the rep if I was lucky enough to get a job. She agreed, thinking I wouldn't be successful, and was shocked when I told her I was off to Oldham,' says Pauline.

Because of the job, she never attended drama school, receiving all the training she needed in rep, where she spent the early years of her career.

As the stage roles grew in significance, Pauline began establishing herself as a noteworthy theatre actress and it was just a matter of time before she made the transition to the small screen – and the opportunity arrived in the late 60s.

'I remember my stage debut, but not my first TV part,' she admits. 'I did all the usual stuff like playing a barrister in *Crown Court* – which I didn't enjoy – and a lot of TV plays that I did.

'I was married to actor Donald Churchill, who I met at Liverpool Rep. He wrote several plays for Armchair Theatre which I appeared in. I was also in a few productions of BBC's *Play for Today*.'

During the 70s, Pauline was kept busy on TV with the series *Harriet's Back in Town*, which ran for a year; the lead in BBC's *A Sentimental Education* and various other productions. She also appeared in *Rumpole of the Bailey*, *Jack's Trade*, *Keep It in the*

they say: "That's it!"'

Pauline's versatility has meant she has worked in all theatrical media, including plenty of theatre work, making her stage debut at the age of 17 as Grace Poole in *Jane Eyre*.

Since those early days, Pauline has notched up over 40 years in the business, though her mother always thought she would eventually turn to a 'respectable' profession.

'Mum believed my desire to act was just a phase I was going through. When I told her I'd been acting 40 years, she couldn't believe it, but still thought I'd change direction and do something different – even at this late stage!'

Surprisingly, Pauline's mum liked the idea of using a hippo to represent Reggie's image of his mother-in-law. 'She loved it. She always came along to watch the recordings and laughed whenever she thought of herself being represented by the hippo – although, of course, it was Elizabeth's mother being portrayed, not her.'

Sadly, the hippo's no longer required for the fourth series, but Pauline's enjoyed bringing the Reggie Perrin saga up to date. 'As usual, filming's gone well and I'm looking forward to seeing the series. It's been hard work but great fun to make and I'm sure it will attract a whole new generation of Reggie Perrin fans.'

Family, playing Muriel Rush, four films, including *She'll Be Wearing Pink Pyjamas* and an Abbey National advert with Richard Wilson.

But even after all this work Pauline is still best remembered for Reggie Perrin, even though it is 20 years since it was screened. 'I obviously look older than when I first played Elizabeth, but people still stop me and say: "I recognise you, now what were you in . . . ?" When I tell them some of my more recent credits, they dismiss them, but as soon as I tell them I played Reggie's wife,

EPISODE THREE:

"I'm not a heat person." (Tom)

One of the funniest episodes in the series finds Reggie scheming for a way of inviting Joan – about whom he is increasingly fantasising – over on Sunday while Elizabeth visits her mother.

On Saturday, while his wife is out shopping, Reggie calls his secretary and tricks her into agreeing to come over by suggesting the future of not just Sunshine Desserts but Reginald Iolanthe Perrin as well, is at stake – something the ever-dependable Joan cannot refuse.

Sunday arrives and Reggie is fretting when Elizabeth seems in no rush to leave and 11 a.m., the agreed time for Joan's arrival, looms.

REGGIE: Come on, darling, come on.
ELIZABETH: Do you know where everything is?

REGGIE: Yes, I think so: the kitchen's through there, and the garden's outside.
ELIZABETH: Reggie!
REGGIE: Well, you do treat me a bit like a child, darling.
ELIZABETH: You are a child.
REGGIE: Yes, I suppose I am. You should have married Henry Possett. Come on, off you go, come on.
ELIZABETH: I didn't want to marry Henry Possett. Oh, there's some aspirin in the medicine cupboard if you get one of your thundery headaches.
REGGIE: Come on, darling, you'll miss your car.
ELIZABETH: You're not listening to a word I say.
REGGIE: Headaches in the medicine cupboard if I have one of my thundery aspirins. Alright? Bye, darling.

Reggie is anxious for Elizabeth to leave

LEFT: **Joan makes her move**
ABOVE: **Reggie causes a diversion while Joan escapes**

His wife's presence is soon replaced by his would-be lover's but not before Reggie has changed his shirt twice following the discovery of long-forgotten BO stains contaminating the armpits, which dents his confidence.

After travelling 20 miles Joan demands to know what the crisis is, so Reggie admits there is not one and he has got her there under false pretences. He apologises profusely and supplies a quick peck on Joan's lips to help compensate. Needing no further encouragement, she leaps at him and uncontrollably smothers Reggie with kisses before dragging him upstairs.

Joan means business and no sooner have they reached the spare bedroom than she slips off her shoes and is attacking Reggie's shirt buttons. But a nervous Reggie is saved by the bell – the door bell – when his rhyming slang talking son, Mark, pops in, followed shortly by Tom and Jimmy.

When Mark decides to go up to the spare bedroom to get some clothes, Reggie has to resort to preventative action by claiming he has secret papers up there for a non-wobble jelly.

When Tom arrives wiping his brow, Mark comments:

MARK: Yeah, 'tis hot, isn't it?
TOM: Very thirst making.
REGGIE: Want a beer do you?
TOM: Oh, thank you. I'm not a heat person. I sweat very freely.
REGGIE: Yes, I had noticed!
TOM: I have very open pores. Lindi squirts sweats quite a bit too – she has very open pores too.

Then Tom wants to visit the spare bedroom to settle a 50p bet he has with Linda about whether one can see the spire of St Peter's Church from the window. Reggie tries desperately to stop him, before rushing upstairs himself. Finding Joan naked in bed, he asks her whether she would make her exit via the drainpipe, making sure she keeps low whilst passing the lounge.

Then the real test begins: while Reggie allows Joan time to escape, he struggles frantically to retain everyone's interest downstairs, nearly blowing several blood vessels in the process. First, out comes a wedding photo; then when a thunder clap draws Jimmy to the window, the highly animated Reggie exhibits a stuffed trout, an empty tube of Nurse Jenkins' wart eradicator and his old cricket scorebook.

Nearing a nervous breakdown, Reggie cannot contain things any longer. Tom and Mark head for the bedroom, by which time Joan has managed to escape, while Jimmy spots a woman crawling through the front garden shrubbery – little did he know it was Joan.

'I REMEMBER' when we were rehearsing the scene where Mark, Tom and Jimmy arrive. The doorbell rang and Len stopped immediately and said: "Is the bell only going to be that loud?" He repeated the question, but still no answer. He then said: "Somebody answer me: is the bell only going to be that loud? If it is we're not going to get a laugh." The floor manager told him it was going to be louder, to which he replied: "Let's hear it then, now!"

'The bell was heard and the scene continued. It was just another example of Len's confidence and desire for getting everything just right. And he was correct, of course. If the bell hadn't been loud enough to startle him or for the audience to hear, he wouldn't have got the same reaction.'

(Geoffrey Palmer)

EPISODE FOUR:

Reggie Perrin, 46, wife away. Strange behaviour. Getting more brazen every day.

"Eleven minutes late, defective axle at Wandsworth." (Reggie)

"I didn't get where I am today by biting people in the changing room!" (C.J.)

Just as Reggie is leaving for work, the phone rings. It is Elizabeth who tells him her mother is still unwell so will be staying over another day; she tells Reggie to cancel the dinner party they had planned with the C.J.s – but Reggie has other ideas!

On the train to work Reggie reluctantly offers Peter Cartwright the Greater Manchester Development Plan Supplement from his newspaper because the sneezer has, once again, forgotten a hankie. He also decides to have some fun: he will not cancel the party, he will just cancel the food.

First task of the day at Sunshine Desserts is to dictate a letter to the Traffic Manager, British Rail (Southern Region).

Tim Barrett

Character: Mr Campbell-Lewiston, sales manager for Sunshine Desserts, Germany.
Series 1, Episode 4.
Born: London.
Credits include: TV – The Dick Emery Show, Terry and June, The Janet Brown Show.
Update: Died at home after a busy TV career.
P.S. Originally known as Arthur Barrett.

Dear Sir,
Despite my letter of Friday last, I see
you have still taken no action in the
matter of the late arrival of trains at
Waterloo. This morning my train
arrived, as always, 11 minutes late.
It is rapidly becoming apparent to me
that not only are you not competent
to hold your job, you could not even
run a game of strip poker in a
Turkish brothel. It should be obvious,
even to a retarded Belgian hamster,
that all your trains should be retimed
to take 11 minutes longer.
        Yours faithfully,
        Reginald I. Perrin

P.S. During the pollen season Peter
Cartwright's sneezing is rather
offensive to those like myself who are
allergic to sneezing. This morning he
blew his nose on the Greater
Manchester Development Plan
Supplement, a sound enough
environmental comment but not a
pretty sight. Why don't you divide
your carriages into sneezers and non-
sneezers?

Next, Reggie decides to ask other guests
to his party: David Harris-Jones; Davina
Letts-Wilkinson from Custards; and his
Uncle Percy Spillinger. He informs Joan the
invitation does not extend to her because
he likes her too much.

Mr Campbell-Lewiston – an employee
working in Sales in Germany – arrives at
Reggie's office saying C.J. had told him he
wanted to see him immediately. Reggie –

employing C.J.'s tactics – asks what time would suit him: Campbell-Lewiston suggests any time that morning, so Reggie states 4.30 the following afternoon. After his visitor has gone, Reggie cannot recall where he has seen him before.

That afternoon, C.J. tells Reggie he wants him to give a speech on the role of luxury desserts in a competitive industrial society at the forthcoming British Fruit Association's Seminar – much to Reggie's delight!

When the guests arrive for what they believe to be a normal, civilised dinner party with nothing but intellectual chitchat, they had not considered the host's current state of mind. Out to shock, Reggie has not informed anyone the menu is blank and that he has carefully selected his guests, particularly Uncle Percy who attracts nothing but glares from the C.J.s with his blue humour and coarse remarks about Davina's oversized bust and 'sturdy pins'!

Eventually, Reggie tells his anguished guests that they will not be getting anything to eat because he feels they live in a world that is far too greedy with not enough food

to go round and instead he will send a £20 cheque to Oxfam.

On the train the following morning, David Harris-Jones – who stayed the night – is nursing a hangover and cannot remember anything of the previous evening, so Reggie takes great delight in telling him.

REGGIE: I said have another drink and you had another seven.
DAVID: Seven!?
REGGIE: Then you asked C.J. for the last waltz.
DAVID: Oh my God!
REGGIE: That was before your trousers came down.
DAVID: My trousers came down?
REGGIE: Yes.
DAVID: I'm wearing my underpants with a picture of Beethoven on them.
REGGIE: Yes, we know.
DAVID: What did C.J. say?
REGGIE: He didn't seem too put out!
DAVID: Oh, good.
REGGIE: He was more worried about Uncle Percy's suggestion that you were probably a poof.

When Reggie arrives at his office, Joan is missing: worried about her boss, she has popped along to ask Doc Morrisey's advice.

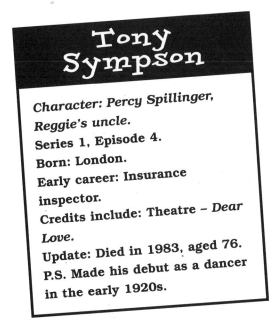

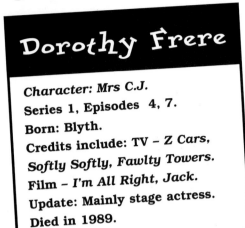

Dorothy Frere

Character: Mrs C.J.
Series 1, Episodes 4, 7.
Born: Blyth.
Credits include: TV – *Z Cars*, *Softly Softly*, *Fawlty Towers*. Film – *I'm All Right, Jack*.
Update: Mainly stage actress.
Died in 1989.

DOC: Ah, Joan. Come in and sit down. Feeling a little chesty? We'll soon have you examined.

JOAN: It isn't about me, Doctor Morrisey.

DOC: Oh, pity. Oh well, can I get you something to drink?

JOAN: Thank you.

DOC: What would you like? Cough mixture, cod liver oil, syrup of figs. . . I've got quite a nice little mouth wash.

JOAN: I don't think I will have a drink after all. It's about Mr Perrin, doctor.

DOC: Ah, yes.

JOAN: Well do you know what's wrong with him?'

DOC: Yes, I do. Middle age exhaustion, boredom, anxiety, self-disgust, misery, self-inferiority, dislike of industry, dislike of instant pudding, 25-year itch, fear, insecurity, frustration.

JOAN: What can we do about it?

DOC: Haven't the faintest idea.

JOAN: There must be something I can do?

DOC: You could try being a little nicer to him, that might help. I say, sure you aren't a little chesty?

JOAN: No!

DOC: Oh. Let me examine you anyway. Go on, do a cartwheel for your uncle.

JOAN: No.

DOC: Joan, don't worry about Reggie. He's

brought things to a crisis, that's good.

JOAN: Is it?

DOC: Oh yes. If I know anything at all about medicine it means he's over the worst.

Before leaving for home, Reggie meets Mr Campbell-Lewiston and after remembering he had bit him in the changing room at school, decides to gain revenge by throwing constant insults under a ruse of a middle management psychology test.

The final scene of the episode reveals a moment of sadness and loneliness, and, perhaps, an early indication of what is to come in the next episode, when Reggie longs to tell Elizabeth how he is missing her, how he is sorry for everything that has happened and for what will happen. He rings her at her mother's but she is annoyed because he has woken her up and poor ol' Reggie does not even get the chance to explain his motivations for calling.

'I REMEMBER . . . it was the first time I'd ever blown my nose in a copy of *The Times*. All my character seemed to do was blow his nose. When John Howard Davies first told me all I had to do was sneeze, I told him it wouldn't be difficult because I had suffered from hay fever since childhood and could sneeze anyway he liked.

'My part was miniscule and didn't really exist outside the carriage scenes, but Peter was a great character and always finished the crossword before Reggie which added to his commuting agonies.

'Playing Peter was wonderful because he was a touch over the top which made him fun, particularly as most of my other roles were starchy, ex-military or legal types. But even in Reggie I didn't quite escape the military trademarks because the wardrobe department went to great pains to find a regimental tie!'

(Terence Conoley)

John Barron

C.J.

The tyrannical C.J. – with his famous catchphrase, 'I didn't get where I am today . . . ' – was Reggie's egocentric boss at Sunshine Desserts. When the jelly giant went bankrupt, C.J. (alias Charles Jefferson) joined Reggie at Grot and later the commune.

After making Reggie Perrin's life hell for 25 years, the tables were turned when, facing life as an unemployed ex-managing director, C.J. was offered the chance of a job by Reggie at Perrins Products (a.k.a. Grot). At the interview, C.J. was subjected to all the annoying and embarrassing acts he once inflicted on others: being kept waiting outside the office door; having to sit on a farting chair; and being promised a small office.

Recruited as the Head of EuroGrot's assistant, C.J. reported to Elizabeth Perrin and was given the boring Miss Erith as secretary. Although Reggie had many scores to settle with his former boss from their days together at Sunshine Desserts, he possessed a well-disguised fondness for the booming authoritarian who did not feel properly dressed without a suit.

When it came to recruiting staff for the commune, C.J. was the first person Reggie tracked down: busking outside a London cinema. Enticed by the promise of a £10K salary and free accommodation – albeit under canvas – C.J. joined as the work therapist.

When the commune closed, C.J. joined

his brother F.J. as Head of Amalgamated Aerosols Air Freshener and Deodorant Division. With roles reversed once again, he hires Reggie Perrin as his number two.

In the new series C.J. still lives in Virginia Water, is 72 years old and retired from industry. His wife lives in Luxembourg full-time.

In a position of power, C.J. signified everything that was wrong with 70s management styles. He was a stickler for offices; liked seeing subordinates squirm in his raspberry-blowing visitors' chairs; hung pictures of himself all over his office walls; and kept visitors waiting outside his door with the saying: '1-2-3-

4, make him sweat outside the door, 5-6-7-8, always pays to make them wait, 9-10-11-12. . . come!' Although his fortunes fluctuated after his redundancy from Sunshine Desserts, he remained the same ol' cliche-ridden C.J.

It was a curious brown parcel that introduced veteran actor John Barron to the world of Reginald Perrin. He was in Manchester filming Granada's *Crown Court,* in which he was one of the resident judges. 'I was working there nearly every week, and one evening I returned to my hotel and found a package waiting for me,' he says.

The unexpected parcel containing a copy of David Nobbs's novel *The Death of Reginald Perrin* had been sent by BBC director John Howard Davies – who produced the pilot – with a note. 'He wanted me to read the book with a view to playing C.J. That evening I read it from cover to cover, and had hardly turned the final page before reaching for the phone to let John Howard Davies know I'd love to accept the role – and that's how it all started.'

It did not take long for John to realise the show was going to be a huge success. Even while filming the pilot – which became episode one when a series was commissioned – he sensed all the essential ingredients were in place: the scripts were not only brilliantly written but extremely funny as well. And every character was suitably shaped for a hit comedy series, including C.J., and John Barron was the ideal candidate for playing the booming lover of clichés.

As well as the obvious satisfaction of being involved in a successful show, playing C. J. gave John the chance to meet up with his old friend, Leonard Rossiter, whom he had known since the 50s. 'I first met Len in 1951 at Preston rep, where he was working as an ASM. Four years later I moved to

direct plays for the repertory company at Wolverhampton – which was viewed as promotion – and Leonard came along as a fully-fledged actor, and it was obvious then that he was going places.

'I like to think I helped him through the early days of his career. People used to ask me how it was we worked so well together; what they didn't know was that we'd known each other for 20 years before Reggie Perrin.'

One reason John Barron enjoyed playing the egotistical boss of Sunshine Desserts was that the character leapt off the printed page particularly well. 'There was a hint in the original book that he was more of a self-made man than I portrayed him, but I don't think that mattered,' explains John. 'One of the charms of the character was that he was always certain he was right, when most of the time he was completely wrong.

'And then, of course, there were all the wonderful clichés that he always got wrong, which David Nobbs built on. It was a great help having David around while we were recording the show, but we hardly had to alter a word which was why rehearsals were such a pleasure. Sometimes with comedies you spend the whole time rewriting – but that never happened. The whole production went so smoothly.'

Born in London on Christmas Eve, 1920, John was brought up by his mother, herself an actress until the arrival of her son. During his schooldays he could not decide how he wanted his future to pan out, so his mother reluctantly suggested he trained to become an actor. 'All she said was she thought I'd better go on the stage and in 1938 persuaded a godfather to pay my fees for RADA, all of £17 a term.

'Luckily, in those days one didn't have to pass much of an entrance test: so long as you could speak the King's English you were home and dry. So I started my acting career before the war which was a great help because later after demob from the navy, I could already class myself as an actor instead of wanting to become one. There were many men who'd gone into the Forces before they'd had a chance to qualify, so when they came out in their late 20s wanting to take up the profession, it was very difficult.'

Like most actors of John's era, his early days were spent in rep. 'In retrospect, I probably spent too much time in rep, but I didn't have any money so couldn't afford to pick and choose,' he says.

It was not long before John became involved in directing various repertory companies, and being offered meatier roles in the West End. Gradually his career took off and he first moved into TV in 1948 in a live theatrical performance from Palmers Green. 'The theatre was conveniently near to Alexandra Palace and its transmitters, so the BBC regularly transmitted live performances which became popular among viewers.'

After several cameos in long-forgotten programmes, John was lucky enough to get a part in ATV's twice-weekly soap, *Emergency-Ward 10*, which led to almost constant employment on the box, usually as upright citizens like chief constables, lawyers, judges and vicars.

During a busy career spanning theatre and TV, John's spent three years playing a chief constable in *Softly Softly*, and has also been the minister in *Doomwatch*; the vicar in *Potter*; the Dean in *All Gas and Gaiters* and a host of other characters in shows like *Whoops Apocalypse*, *To the Manor Born*, *The Foundation*, *Yes, Minister*, *Department S*, *The Saint*, *No Place Like Home* and *Don't Wait Up*.

He's also made several films, including: *The Day the Earth Caught Fire* in 1961, *Jigsaw* and *The Italian Secret Service*.

About five years ago, John moved from London to Sussex, where he now lives, to take things a little easier. Since then he has not done much notable TV work and has dedicated his time to working in the theatre.

Looking back almost six decades in the business, John does not hesitate in selecting the best compliment he has received during his career. 'Middle-aged parents kept coming up to me saying: "You ruined my life because my child wouldn't stop saying, 'I didn't get where I am today without . . ."' Playing C.J. has been the highlight of my television career.'

John Barron in
Whoops
Apocalypse

EPISODE FIVE:

"Eleven minutes late, somebody had stolen the lines at Surbiton." (Reggie)

"I didn't get where I am today by saying earwig instead of thank you." (C.J.)

Reggie, who has begun calling things earwig and thinking of C.J. as a toothbrush, confides in Ponsonby, his cat, before leaving for work one Friday morning. Not only will he surprise everyone while addressing the British Fruit Association later that day, but he plans ruining C.J.'s weekend fishing contest before slipping off into the sunset marking the end of Reginald Iolanthe Perrin. His last day as the bored, middle-aged, directionless, executive has finally arrived.

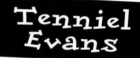

Tenniel Evans

Character: Elwyn Watkins, chief scientific adviser, Bridgend College of Pesticides.
Series 1, Episode 5.
Born: Nairobi.
Training: RADA.
Credits include: TV – No Hiding Place, The Sullivan Brothers, Bergerac.
Update: Qualified as clergyman in 1986, having trained in the evenings.

Dennis Ramsden

Character: Dr Hump, lecturer in the philosophy of fruit.
Series 1, Episode 5.
Born: Leeds.
Credits include: TV – Robin's Nest, George and Mildred, Only Fools and Horses, To the Manor Born.
Update: Now concentrating on theatrical directing.
P.S. Started acting in the RAF. TV career began in children's shows.

Before he leaves for work, Elizabeth asks Reggie what time she should arrive for the speech.

ELIZABETH: You seem rather on edge this morning, are you nervous about your speech?
REGGIE: No, no, I'm alright, darling. I've just got a bit of an earwig that's all. Headache, headache.
ELIZABETH: What time should I arrive at the hall for the lunch?
REGGIE: Oh, about half past parsnips. Sorry, darling, twelve, twelve, half past twelve.
ELIZABETH: Yes, but where do parsnips come in?
REGGIE: Yes, I just remembered C.J. asked me if I could get hold of a few parsnips for him.
ELIZABETH: What on earth does he want parsnips for?
REGGIE: He didn't say.

On his way to work Reggie smiles to

himself as he realises this will be his last trip on the train with all the faceless people and listening to Peter Cartwright's hay fever symptoms. He then throws his briefcase out of the window.

After wishing Joan good luck for the future and telling her how much he values her friendship, which worries her because it sounds too much like a farewell speech,

Reggie goes off and gets drunk.

For lunch Reggie meets Elizabeth, Dr Hump (a lecturer in the philosophy of fruit at the University of Budleigh Salterton) and the seminar chairman, Mr Watkins (chief

Elizabeth tells Reggie she is worried about him

scientific adviser, Bridgend College of Pesticides).

Eventually it is speech time. An inebriated Reggie splutters through his speech getting progressively worse and less decipherable until he is bundled off stage and thrown out of the hall.

While Elizabeth drives her dejected husband home he stops off to visit the loo, but uses the opportunity to run off in his quest to relieve himself of the burdens associated with life as Reggie Perrin.

After borrowing a truck from Sunshine Desserts, Reggie heads for the south coast via C.J.'s country residence – the venue of the weekend's fishing competition – where he ruins the contest by releasing loganberry juice into the river which C.J., Doc Morrisey, David and Tony mistake for blood.

That evening, Reggie, dressed in his suit and clutching a suitcase, stares out on the cold, moonlit sea and contemplates suicide to prove he is not a fraud. Realising the water is too cold, he decides instead to slip on an artificial wig and beard, and tour the countryside with a new identity.

'I REMEMBER Reggie Perrin was my only real experience of working with Leonard. What astounded me was his incredible memory for learning lines – especially during the drunken speech scene. The episode took about a week to rehearse, but by the second day Leonard had already discarded the script and learnt his lines and moves.' **(Dennis Ramsden)**

John Rudling

Character: Bill, security, Sunshine Desserts.
Series 1, Episode 5.
Born: London.
Early career: Draughtsman.
Credits include: TV – To the Manor Born (Brabinger).
Film – The Ladykillers, The Man in the White Suit.
Update: Died in 1983.

Charmian May

Character: Miss Pershore.
Series 1, Episodes 6, 7.
Born: Hampshire.
Training: RADA.
Credits include: TV – You're Only Young Twice, Don't Wait Up, Soldier, Soldier.
Update: Wrote and directed one-woman show, Celebrating Shakespeare in UK and USA.
P.S. Spent fifteen years in rep before TV debut.

Reggie in the office he can no longer bear to work in

EPISODE SIX:

Reggie Perrin, 46, has disappeared, clothes found abandoned on beach. Presumed dead. Still very much alive.

"I didn't get where I am today by thinking!" (C.J.)

For a brief moment in his life Reggie enjoys his newly-found freedom. Under disguise amid the Dorset countryside he can go anywhere and be whoever he likes.

After rejecting several guises, Reggie pops into a pub in a village where he spent many summer holidays and gets chatting to the barmaid, Rosie. Reggie boasts that his first girlfriend was from the village and they used to go up lovers' lane together. The lane has since been turned into a neo-Georgian detached house.

Reggie decides it is time to dash when he remembers out loud another girl from the past who was always riding horses, was very large and nervous. Unfortunately, this turns out to be the barmaid. Reggie decides it is time to leave.

Whilst drinking on a terrace at another pub, under the pseudonym Lord Amhurst: mountaineer, explorer, cement tycoon, band leader, gourmet and sex maniac, Reggie gets chatting to Jean Timpkins at the next table

who believes she recognises him as Lord Amhurst. When she invites him back to her house Reggie stares into space and imagines the cosy scene of him and Elizabeth snuggling up on the settee – the life he so foolishly left behind.

His brief excursion away from being Reggie Perrin has brought much pain, expecially to the ones he has left behind, but at this moment it may all have been worth it because, perhaps, for the first time in a very long while he realises he loves Elizabeth and shudders when he thinks what it would be like without her in his life. Now he must return to his suburban existence: the problem is how?

He returns disguised initially as a Welshman and pops into the local pub near Sunshine Desserts to find C.J., David and Tony chatting about him. When C.J. asks what they thought of Reggie, David stutters:

DAVID: I think he was a bit unpredictable; he wasn't always unpredictable, sometimes he was very predictable. But you could never predict when he was going to be predictable, an-n-n-d when he was going to be . . .unpredictable.
TONY: Quite frankly, I think he was a decent enough chap who just wasn't up to it.

Reggie's heard enough and leaves. He walks back home along the once familiar streets feeling deeply depressed, questioning what he has done. Now, he is all alone: no

---

Reggie's beloved daughter and wife – the family he left behind

friends, family or job. He decides he must see Elizabeth again to show her he loves her, but a neighbour tells him she has gone to Worthing to see her mother in hospital.

Dressed up as an Italian tourist wearing black glasses, a quiff-shaped wig and a large set of false teeth, Reggie waits for her at the railway station only to see her emerge with Henry Possett. He scrounges a lift but knows this is not the right time to confide in his wife.

His next disguise is as scruffy Donald Potts. Straggly-haired, goofy-teethed, Reggie applies for a job in the local council's Parks Department. The guffawing personnel officer, Mr Thorneycroft, is exceptionally pleased when he discovers Donald has no references, is unemployed and has served six months for embezzlement. Reggie is offered a job, not in the local parks, but at the North Hillingly Sewerage Reclamation Works.

Back at his digs – which are owned by the weird Mr and Mrs Deacon – Reggie rereads the letter he has been planning to send to Elizabeth explaining the troubles he faces in his life, but realises he cannot post it, so rips it up. It is a shame because what a letter . . .

Dear Elizabeth,
I have been here a week and I still haven't finished writing this letter. I found the routine of my job very difficult at first, but now I'm falling in with it.

David Millet

Character: Landlord.
Series 1, Episode 6.

Pamela Manson

Character: Barmaid.
Series 1, Episode 6.
Born: London.
Early career: PR in fashion industry, secretary and theatrical agent.
Credits include: TV – Are You Being Served?, Dad's Army, The Professionals.
Update: Died in 1988, aged 59.

My landlady seems very nice. I often miss you but I know I could never again offer you the support that you need. I can't believe in the expansion of industry, the challenge of the Common Market, any of the claptrap – so much seems ridiculous. The shape of this pen seems ridiculous; I can't take the male sexual organ seriously, the sight of a pumice stone is liable to drive me hysterical and I shall never again be able to look at your mother without thinking of a hippopotamus: I just did and it was lovely.

I had to leave you darling. I felt as if I was going sane and mad at the same time. But then the words sane and mad don't have much meaning, do they? So few words do: blue, green, butter, kettle. Even blue is green to some people, and others can't tell the difference between butter and margarine.

Oh my darling, Elizabeth. We never talked enough or loved enough, or lived enough. When did I last tell you I loved you? Which I do so very much.

It's hard to know that I will never see you again, and I can't even send you this letter, and that you'll never receive my best wishes for the future and how much I love you.

Your ever loving Reggie.

Bob Sutherland

Character: Major.
Series 1, Episode 6.

Before the evening is out, Miss Pershore – who also has digs there – pesters Reggie until, getting a little too friendly, he ushers her out of his room.

The following day, Reggie cannot stand his predicament a minute longer and decides to reveal his identity to Linda, which – as expected – comes as a great shock. He coaxes his daughter into telling Elizabeth – who is visiting Linda shortly – that he is still alive, but before she can her mother breaks the news of her engagement to Henry Possett.

'I REMEMBER a lot of people kept telling me how much they liked Miss Pershore. Luckily, I don't look anything like her. One

Hilary Mason

Character: Mrs Deacon.
Series 1, Episode 6.
Born: Birmingham.
Training: London School of Dramatic Art.
Early career: Shorthand typist.
Credits include: TV – Bergerac, David Copperfield, Don't Look Now, The Detectives, Casualty.

of the beauties of make-up is that you can be made to look pretty dreadful. I played a lot of odd, spinster types, especially on stage, so it wasn't a hard role to get into. Leonard was wearing a wig during the scenes I had with him, and he kept reminding me of it and saying: "Make sure you mind my wig.'

(Charmian May)

'I didn't even appear on the credits for my first appearance in the series. I ended up spending the day kissing Leonard Rossiter in a car before I'd even had chance to speak to him – it was quite amusing.

'The episode was filmed on location and I was told I was involved in a flashback of an old girlfriend, with the scene being filmed in an old-fashioned car on the front lawn of this newly built detached house.

'When I arrived on set Leonard was already in the car, so the producer sat me in the vehicle and said: "Kiss him!" We hadn't even said hello before we were involved in this great snogging session. About half an hour later we had a chat.

'It was such a small part that I couldn't

believe when I started getting fan letters. That just goes to show how popular the series was.'

(Helen Bernat)

Geoffrey Palmer

JIMMY ANDERSON

Militaristic Jimmy – who drove his first wife, Sheila, to drink, and lost his second, Lettuce, in an accident – was a Major in the Queen's Own Berkshire Light Infantry before being booted out under the guise of 'early retirement'.

His life was one endless failure: he was expelled from Harrow, and the founder of several crackpot schemes such as a private army – until his supposed top-drawer colleague scarpered with all the equipment and money. He then ventured into the world of narrow boat hire until he was again taken for a ride.

Although he was admirable in some ways, and was always full of good intentions, nothing ever went right for Jimmy. He was a sad figure, somewhat aloof from the world around him. He was also the world's biggest sponger, using visits to see his sister, Elizabeth, as a chance to scrounge some groceries because he experienced a 'bit of a cock up on the catering front!'

When his secret army plans collapsed, Jimmy joined Reggie at Grot as Head of Creative Thinking, at the time Reggie was recruiting people for jobs for which they were totally unsuitable.

Later when Perrins (the commune) was established, Jimmy – who spoke in clipped military lingo – was setting up his narrow boat business, but soon came running to Reggie for a job when it folded. He was placed in charge of the unit of good works: picking up litter,

helping old ladies across the road, etc.

When the commune closed Jimmy had plans for a joint venture with an old friend, Nigel 'Ginger' Carstairs, who owned a chair lift in Switzerland.

It took some time before Geoffrey Palmer knew how to play Elizabeth's brother, Jimmy, when he appeared in episode two.

'He was a difficult character to get to grips with,' says Geoffrey, 'and I remember during rehearsals Leonard saying: "It's not going to work if you play it like that!" Gradually I realised the character had to be

stronger and bigger in his blundering incompetence – he couldn't be bland.

'It was a great pleasure to be in Reggie Perrin. You had one enormous central character surrounded by a group of wonderful, diverse supporting characters and it worked very well.'

Geoffrey describes himself as an over-the-top actor during the early part of his career, but Reggie Perrin marked a turning point because ever since he has tried successfully to be more subtle, economical and realistic in his acting.

'Once I established the character, I enjoyed playing Jimmy, who, along with everybody else, was larger than life with a brain that was ready to explode. 'But there was always a germ of truth and reality in Reggie and the rest of them. Take Jimmy: he's a sad failure in every way but is full of good intentions. He tries to be a public schoolboy and an officer but fails in both.'

Geoffrey was amazed at how quickly the series became a hit. 'Everyone felt it was going to work, but no one could believe just how successful it became,' he says.

'I quickly began looking forward to going to work and it was one of the happiest projects I've worked on. At that time there was an awful lot of rubbish being made, and

Reggie and brother-in-law, Jimmy, played by Geoffrey Palmer

although one was grateful for a job, you always hoped that you'd get the added bonus of the programme being a quality product and enjoyable – and I got that with Reggie.'

The Jimmy character became so popular that David Nobbs wrote a spin-off series, *Fairly Secret Army,* in which Geoffrey played Major Harry Truscott, a right-winger who formed his own army to safeguard the country from the loony left.

One day while filming the third series of Reggie, David told Geoffrey about his plans for the series, which met with nothing but enthusiasm. After initially showing interest, the BBC shied away from commissioning the project, believing it was politically incorrect. But David was successful in attracting the support of Channel 4, who transmitted two series in 1984 and '86.

When Geoffrey learnt about the new Reggie Perrin series he was very wary and it took a lot of persuasion before he decided to get involved. 'David Nobbs called me because he'd heard of my concerns regarding reviving the series. We had a good chat and after he told me about his plans, I agreed to do it.'

But Geoffrey still harboured concerns when filming began. 'I just felt the Press would say: "Haven't the BBC, David Nobbs or the actors got anything better to do than bring back something that was a success 20 years ago?"

'The challenge facing the new series is that you cannot possibly do better than the first and second series of Reggie with the same characters but without the leading man,' says Geoffrey. But now the fourth series has been completed, he believes the series may be strong enough to attract a whole new audience.

Geoffrey – the son of a chartered surveyor – grew up in London and was educated at Highgate School. After completing national service he joined civvy street with no idea what he wanted from life and found himself working in an exports office for nine months.

'In a way it was a bit like Reggie's predicament because I quickly got bored and realised I couldn't work in the office until I was 65, so decided to do something about it.'

After leaving his job, Geoffrey found himself still unsure what to do and ended up in another office, this time courtesy of a friend's invitation to join his father's accountancy office. But boredom soon returned.

At the same time, a girlfriend had persuaded Geoffrey to join the local amateur dramatics society, which he enjoyed. Taking the advice of a professional actor, he decided to give acting a go, becoming an unpaid trainee ASM at the Q Theatre in London – which, sadly, no longer exists.

After 18 months, Geoffrey moved to Croydon's Grand Theatre as a qualified ASM, which offered him the chance of playing small parts. Several years of rep and touring followed before he made the inevitable step into the world of TV. 'I did an enormous amount of TV in the early days and worked a lot with comics in live sketches, including Arthur Askey, Dickie Valentine, Harry Worth, Harry Secombe and Jimmy James.'

Then Geoffrey started making one-off appearances in a range of early productions, including *Shadow Squad* in 1957; Granada's *Skyport* with John Horsley in 1960 and ITV's early police series *No Hiding Place*. His first regular part was in *Family Solicitor* during the 60s.

Since, he has become one of TV's most popular actors, with a memorable guest appearance in *Fawlty Towers*, and leading roles in the long-running classic *Butterflies*,

alongside Wendy Craig; Donald Fairchild in *Executive Stress*; Harold Stringer in *Hot Metal*; Alan Ayckbourn's *Absurd Person Singular* and *Season's Greetings*; Alan Bennett's *Insurance Man* and *A Question of Attribution*. He also played Lionel in five series of *As Time Goes By* with Dame Judi Dench.

Nowadays Geoffrey prefers working in TV to the theatre. 'The stage doesn't appeal so much now because I don't fancy giving up six nights a week, nine months a year,' he says. 'I'm quite content settling for TV.'

Geoffrey Palmer as Major Harry Truscott in *Fairly Secret Army*

EPISODE SEVEN:

Reggie Perrin, 46. Presumed dead, reveals identity to daughter. Wishes to return to wife, but wife engaged to Henry Possett. Oh, misery! Reggie Perrin heavily disguised.

"I didn't get where I am today without knowing there isn't any fun in getting where I am today!" (C.J.)

Reggie adopts what turns out to be a more longstanding disguise, as the curly-haired, bearded Martin Wellbourne, to attend his own memorial service. Seated at the back of the church, he notices the disappointing turnout.

Outside the church, Martin tries slipping away but Elizabeth spots him and after he tells her he was an old friend of Reggie's who lost touch because he lived in Brazil, she invites him back to the house where family and friends are gathering after the

Reggie disguised as Martin Wellbourne

funeral. For the first time since his faked suicide, he apprehensively meets his family and old colleagues.

Introduced as various names: Mervyn Wishbone, Melvyn Windscreen, Melville Windpipe and Melvyn Washroom, when Jimmy meets him he believes Martin comes from Peru.

JIMMY: I've often wanted to know what it's like in Peru in winter?
REGGIE: Brazil.
JIMMY: Really, like Brazil?
REGGIE: I was in Brazil, not Peru.
JIMMY: Sorry, memory like a sieve; could have sworn Tom said Peru.
REGGIE: No, Tom said the Argentine, but it was Brazil.
JIMMY: Oh – what's it like in Brazil in the winter?
REGGIE: Chilly!

At the house Elizabeth suddenly notices Martin for what he really is: Reggie in disguise, but she does not let on. Before he leaves, Elizabeth invites Martin for a drive in the country to show him around the area.

During the afternoon drive, Martin tells Elizabeth everything she would ever want to know about Brazil, just as if he was reading it from an encyclopedia. Back at home,

David Warwick as Mark

Elizabeth tells Martin it is just like being with Reggie and tells him she has broken off the engagement with Henry Possett.

Increasingly, Martin begins giving away little details which nearly blow his patchy disguise. Elizabeth plays on this and in many ways enjoys seeing Martin squirm as he tries wriggling out of the deep holes he keeps digging for himself.

Before the day ends, Martin asks Elizabeth to marry him. When she accepts, he moves back into his old house and Elizabeth arranges a job interview for Martin at Sunshine Desserts.

Soon he is re-employed to coordinate The Reginald Perrin Memorial Foundation, a scheme C.J. is introducing – to everyone's surprise – to ensure his workforce is happy. Joan is assigned as his new secretary and his immediate boss is Tony Webster.

That evening, Elizabeth and Martin announce their forthcoming marriage to the family. While in the kitchen Linda tells Elizabeth that Martin is really Reggie, which she admits to knowing but says she will not tell anyone because Reggie was unhappy as Reggie and seems much happier as Martin. Little does she know that the deceit is beginning to eat away at him.

'I REMEMBER it was a busy time for my career when I began playing Mark. During the day I played Leonard Rossiter's son, and Gerald Harper's on stage during the evening in my first West End production. It was a great couple of weeks.

'Whenever I watch the epsiodes now I can't believe how I looked. I'd grown long hair and a beard for my theatre role and when I arrived to record Reggie, some of the crew were worried I'd look too much like Tim Preece. They asked whether I'd cut my hair and shave off my beard, but I couldn't because of the play!'

(David Warwick)

Gerald Sim

Character: Vicar.
Series 1, Episode 7.
Born: Liverpool.
Training: RADA.
Credits include: TV – *Edward and Mrs Simpson, Miss Marple, To the Manor Born, The Foundation.*
Film: *Whistle Down the Wind, A Bridge Too Far.*
Update: Appears in fourth series as vicar who buries Reggie.
P.S. Brother of actress Sheila Sim.

Peter MacKriel

Character: Waiter.
Credited in Series 1, Episode 7, scene cut.
Born: Wolverhampton.
Early career: Ministry of Agriculture and Fisheries.
Credits include: *As Time Goes By, Never the Twain, The Bill, Lovejoy, Boon.*

John Forbes Robertson

Character: Henry Possett.
Series 1, Episodes 6, 7.
Born: Worthing.
Credits include: TV – *Dixon of Dock Green, Poldark, The Naked Civil Servant, The New Avengers.*
Film – *Carve Her Name With Pride, The Vampire Lovers.*
P.S. Played Hammer's last Count Dracula.

SERIES TWO:

'Grot-A Load of
Old Rubbish'

EPISODE ONE:

"Seventeen minutes late, water seeping through the cables at Effingham." (Reggie)

"I didn't get where I am today trusting the easy chairs!" (C.J.)

Reggie is fed up being Martin Wellbourne and realises it is time to own up, especially

Reggie - The master of disguise

Reginald Perrin

when he begins slipping into all of Reggie's old habits like staring at Joan's legs and reporting the reason for his lateness upon arriving at his office - although the delay has extended six minutes since the first series.

   As part of C.J.'s new drive to appear caring and understanding towards his employees, he has got Martin carrying out regular monthly chats with his subordinates. Arriving for his session is David Harris-Jones, just as diffident as ever.

(David knocks on Martin's door)
MARTIN: Come in.
(David knocks again)
MARTIN: Come in!

Reggie is re-united with his family at last

DAVID: Sorry, I-I-I-I wasn't sure whether I heard you say come in or not, so I thought if you didn't I'd better not a-a-a-nd if you did you'd say it again a-a-a-nd I could always come in then.

Keeping up the Martin Wellbourne pretence is becoming unbearable for Reggie as well as impractical, as my favourite scene from the entire three series shows. While taking an evening stroll with Elizabeth, Reggie gets an attack of the extraordinarily rare indigestion of the face.

ELIZABETH: Reggie never wanted to go for a walk in the evenings.
MARTIN: But I'm so different from him, darling. God it's coming off!
(Martin holds his beard.)
ELIZABETH: What is it?
MARTIN: Oh, it's indigestion, darling.'
ELIZABETH: In the face?
MARTIN: Yes. I keep getting these attacks of indigestion in the face.
(Martin runs off to the nearest tree.)
ELIZABETH: Can I help?
MARTIN: No! No, please. I like to be on my own when I get these indigestion face attacks. Ah, that's it, I feel better now, darling. (Martin adjusts his beard.)

The following day at work C.J. tells Martin he is re-employing Doc Morrisey because he realises the importance of loyalty and happiness. Surely, this new caring

image portrayed by C.J. cannot last much longer?

That evening, Reggie reveals his true identity to Elizabeth and the family. They all welcome him home, including priggish Tom, once he has aired his views on

Ken Barker

Character: GPO Engineer.
Series 2, Episode 1.
Born: London.
Credits include: TV – Z Cars,
Dixon of Dock Green, New
Scotland Yard, Last of the
Summer Wine.
Film (stuntman) – Superman,
Indiana Jones, Octopussy.
P.S. Swimmer in opening
credits.

wasting 50p in the memorial fund.

The next day, Reggie wears his wig and beard for the last time to work. But it is not long before Joan admits to knowing that Martin is really Reggie. To make matters worse, during a medical Doc Morrisey also realises Martin is Reggie in disguise.

Doc: And your name is?
Martin: Martin Wellbourne.
Doc: Well take your clothes off and put them over there on top of mine.
Martin: Right. (Starts to take coat off) What?
Doc: Oh, it's just a joke to put the patients at ease.
Martin: Oh, I see.
Doc: I've been brushing up on psychology.
Martin: Right.
Doc: While I've been on the dole. Open wide. You run this – say ah – Reginald Perrin Memorial whatsit, don't you?
Martin: Yes, that is abso – ah – lutely correct.
Doc: How's it go . . . – and again – going well is it?
Martin: Well, I don't think – ah – people want to be happy really.
Doc: Shirt up. How many people – say 99 – are you dealing with?

Martin: Oh, about two hundred – 99 – and six.
Doc: Quite a task. Yes, it's against nature – deep breath – to be happy at work.
Martin: Well, I've always thought – deep breath – so, yes.

When the Doc discovers that beneath the curly wig and beard is none other than Reggie, he flies off to tell C.J., who has already given up being nice to staff and sacks them both.

Left with no alternative, Reggie returns to the piggery.

'I REMEMBER while filming the scene of Doc Morrisey examining Martin Wellbourne, John Horsley kept the stethoscope round his neck the entire time. He forgot to stick the earpieces in his ears and no one noticed, except the audience.

'John's a wonderful actor but struggles a little when he's got to act and use props at the same time. He's the only actor who'll say: "Go over there!" and then use the gesture.'

(Gareth Gwenlan)

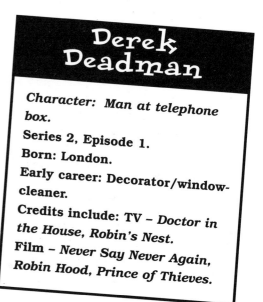

Derek Deadman

Character: Man at telephone box.
Series 2, Episode 1.
Born: London.
Early career: Decorator/window-cleaner.
Credits include: TV – Doctor in the House, Robin's Nest.
Film – Never Say Never Again, Robin Hood, Prince of Thieves.

Tim Preece

TOM PATTERSON
(SERIES 1, 2 & 4)

Estate agent Tom – husband to Reggie's daughter Linda, who he continually referred to as 'Lindyscoop, Floppysquirts, and similar terms of endearment – was a role model in pomposity. With his lugubrious face, open pores and lack of humour, he was a first-class bore who tortured the Perrin family with revolting homemade wines that became bestsellers in Grot. Poor ol' Tom did not have a lot going for him and was constantly insulted by Reggie, who called him a 'pompous prig'.

With his catchphrase, 'I'm not a . . . person', the bespectacled, pipe-smoking Tom wore a straggly beard in the first series, just a bushy moustache in the second, and is completely shaven for the new series.

His career in estate agency involved writing supposedly witty house adverts for the *Cookham and Thames Ditton Chronicle.* This so-called skill was further tapped when he worked as Grot's Head of Publicity. Tom later joined the commune as the sports therapist with the objective of eliminating competition and aggression from sport. He was completely unsuitable for both jobs, which is what Reggie intended. When the commune collapsed Tom returned to the world of house-selling.

By the fourth series, Tom – divorced from Linda – has recently been made redundant from estate agents Wilmot and Pargetter. His children, Jocasta and Adam, are touring Asia and working for the BBC respectively. By the end of the series, Tom and Linda remarry.

Tim Preece – perfectly cast as Tom – tried desperately to summon up a short, round fellow from within upon reading the Reggie Perrin scripts. But he realised the task was impossible, which is hardly surprising considering the lanky actor is over six feet tall.

'I never thought I was right for the part of Tom because to me he should've been round and fat. In the end I decided to play it the way that suited my style, admits Tim, who knew both Leonard Rossiter and producer Gareth Gwenlan before appearing in Reggie.

'I first worked with Len at the Bristol Old Vic in One Way Pendulum in 1960. He was the leading actor while I, being only a drama student, had a very small part. Over the years we became good friends and with his encouragement, I even tried writing for him.'

Tim has since had success as a writer with two TV plays already to his credit, one earning him a nomination for 'best newcomer' by the Writer's Guild; but he remembers being very green when he began writing. 'I recall many abortive attempts at satirical sketches for Len in the early 60s. Even though he was always kind about my work, I realise now how awful they were.

'As for Gareth, I met him on a series shortly before Reggie called *Making Faces*, which was filmed at Pebble Mill. Tragically, like many of the earlier BBC programmes, all the episodes have been wiped which is a shame because it was a splendid show. Since then I've worked for him often, including three years playing the vicar in *Waiting for God.*'

After two successful Reggie Perrin series, Tim was saddened when a prior contract meant he was unavailable for the third series, the part being offered to Leslie Schofield instead. What made the agony worse was that the series Tim did flopped.

'It was called *The Deep Concern* and was awful,' he says. 'There was no way I could get out of it which felt like a tragedy.'

One of Tim's favourite memories of Reggie was working with a wonderful cast. 'We got to know each other so well it felt like one big happy family. Some of us invented a one stump cricket game which we played on location whenever we had a spare moment. Trevor Adams, like me, was a cricket fanatic and enjoyed having a game.'

When Tim read about the possibility of a fourth series in an article in *The Guardian* he could hardly believe it and phoned Gareth Gwenlan to see if it was true. 'I'm very excited by it all and think the series will be a great success when it's screened. At least I don't have to wear those awful safari suits Tom wore back in the 70s,' laughs Tim. 'I watch old episodes in horror because he epitomised the worst kind of fashion from that era.'

Tim has also enjoyed meeting up with David Nobbs again after so long. 'Reggie

Perrin was a brilliant creation, and one of David's masterstrokes was the invention of so many catchphrases people remember even to this day. I was taking a train to London a few months ago and got talking with a man who turned to me and said: "I'm not a train person!"'

Born in Shropshire, Tim acted in school plays while studying the Classics, Latin, Greek and Ancient History. After failing to get into Cambridge in 1956, he headed for Bristol. 'A friend said I should go to a university where I could enjoy myself and suggested the Classics and Drama course at Bristol. It was the first of its kind so I applied and was offered a place – and thoroughly enjoyed it.'

After a brief spell at Whitby rep, Tim returned for a year's drama course at Bristol's Old Vic Theatre School. From there he resumed his stage career at Salisbury and Farnham, where he was spotted and offered his first taste of West End theatre.

His TV debut was a small part as a policeman being hit over the head on the *Arthur Haynes Show*, followed by an appearance in *Mr Pastry's Progress*. The occasional rep mingled with plenty of work in the West End and on TV followed until Tim progressed to leading and key supporting roles in a host of programmes. His busy TV career has included roles in *Brookside, Eastenders, Just William* (three episodes), *Waiting for God, Porterhouse Blue. Growing Rich* and *Take Me Home* with Keith Barron.

Although Tim has always received solid support from his family he believes there was always a feeling – which he experienced himself – that his excursion into acting would only be temporary.

'For a while I felt acting would be a short-term measure, something I'd do while I was still 'young'. By the time I was 30 even I thought I'd retrain as a teacher or try to

Tim Preece as Tom Patterson with Reggie

become a politician,' laughs Tim, 'but here I am years later still enjoying life as an actor.'

Looking back over Tim's busy career it is interesting that most of his work has been in drama – surprising for an actor with such a talent for comedy. 'It's just the way the cookie crumbles I suppose,' he explains. 'I've done a lot of drama and even the odd presenting job, such as Landshapes, a programme on geomorphology, for Channel 4. But it'll take a lot to beat Reggie because that was just a joy to do. In my opinion the second series improved on what was already a brilliant first series. David managed to move the series on, and also managed the trick of knowing when to stop. Often there's a tendency to get as much as one can out of an idea, but by stopping while the show was at the top, it's made a compact package that has been repeated so regularly it's become famous – and now there'll be a fourth series to add to that classic collection.'

EPISODE TWO:

Reggie's true identity revealed. Sacked by Sunshine Desserts. Working at pig farm.

"I didn't get where I am today making room for broken reeds, lame ducks or stool pigeons."(C.J.)

"What the eye doesn't see is goose for the gander." (C.J.)

Reggie packs in his job at the piggery – much to Mr Pelham's regret – and looks unsuccessfully for alternative employment. After 130 rejection letters, Elizabeth gives her husband an ultimatum: if he does not find a job by the end of the week she will go out to work. This hurts Reggie's male pride so he heads off for the labour exchange.

Whilst being interviewed by the clerk, Reggie begins realising that his faked suicide phase has become something of a burden while job-hunting. Meanwhile, Elizabeth decides to get a job regardless, and secures a secretarial role reporting to Tony Webster and David Harris-Jones at Sunshine Desserts.

Deciding to shield the true identity of the

Reggie looks for a job

company employing her, Elizabeth tells Reggie she works for the British Basket Company. As frequently happens in the series, roles reverse and next morning, Reggie – wearing a pinny – sees Elizabeth off to work.

REGGIE: Off you go then darling, mustn't be late for your first day. Besides, I want to get down the shops before the crowds.
REGGIE: Umbrella.
ELIZABETH: Thank you, darling.
REGGIE: Handbag.
ELIZABETH: Thank you, darling.
REGGIE: Mirror.
ELIZABETH: Oh yes.
REGGIE: Have a nice day at the office.
(They kiss.)
ELIZABETH: I won't.

   Over the next few days, Reggie's suspicions of where Elizabeth works deepen. His own working life is rather

place of work. Surprise, surprise, it is Sunshine Desserts.

"I REMEMBER Leonard was probably the fastest actor I've ever worked with. I loved playing Mr Pelham. In those days I was always cast as coppers, so to play a country pig farmer was enormous fun. A few of the scenes Leonard and I did were with the pigs and they always gave us a rough time.

'It was a happy company to work with: all the cast were friendly and I found Gareth Gwenlan and David Nobbs very helpful. I feel they were an actor's director and actor's writer because they were always approachable and would listen to your ideas. 'It's certainly one of my favourite roles. I think it was so successful because it was fresh and different. So many stories follow a trodden line but David created a unique idea that was bound to be successful.'

(Glynn Edwards)

capricious. After being employed by Tom as a trainee estate agent, he gets the sack for outbidding a client, which leaves him no choice but to return to the pig farm.

The closing scene of the episode shows Reggie – who by now suspects Elizabeth of having an affair – following his wife to her

Helen Bernat

Characters: Girl kissing Reggie & girl at bus stop.
Series 1, Episode 6 (uncredited).
Series 2, Episode 2.
Born: London.
Training: Italia Conti School.
Credits include: TV – *Some Mothers Do 'Ave 'Em, The goodies.*
Update: Now runs a beauty salon and hairdressers.
P.S. Joined dancing school aged three.

Christopher Lawrence

Character: House buyer.
Series 2, Episode 2.
Born: Liverpool.
Early career: Tyre fitter and musician.
Credits include: TV – *Brookside, Emmerdale.*
Update: Died in 1991, aged 59.
P.S. Enjoyed a successful career as a mandolin player and comic.

Ralph Watson

Character: Labour exchange clerk.
Series 2, Episode 2.

The roles are reversed as Reggie stays at home

EPISODE THREE:

Reggie working at pig farm. Elizabeth at Sunshine Desserts. Reggie suspects Elizabeth of having an affair with C.J.

"I didn't get where I am today by having two black eyes!" (C.J.)

"There's no smoke without the worm turning." (C.J.)

Not only has Reggie unearthed the reasons for Elizabeth's secrecy regarding her job, but he also believes she is having an affair with C.J. (who by now is talking increasingly in clichés) – which is the reason she worked the previous Saturday.

After following his wife to Sunshine Desserts Reggie storms into C.J.'s office demanding Elizabeth is sacked. But before he can tell C.J. what he has planned for him, his ex-boss says: 'Careful, Reggie. Tony's only a young man.' C.J. suggests it is Tony Webster he should be concerned about.

Outside Sunshine Desserts Reggie waits for his victim. When Tony appears Reggie swears and assaults the would-be whizz kid. Joan arrives on the scene and reveals her allegiance to Tony instead of the now out of favour Reggie, when she runs over to help Tony. Joan's feelings towards Reggie are now primarily those of friendship, not passion.

At the piggery the following day, Reggie - who looks rather conspicuous with the two black eyes he earned from the previous day's fight - is asked into the office. Mr Pelham thinks it is strange Reggie has two shiners when he was supposedly visiting his auntie. How can Reggie get out of this one?

MR PELHAM: You seem to have rubbed your auntie up the wrong way?
REGGIE: What auntie is that, Mr P?
MR PELHAM: When you took yesterday off you said your auntie was ill.
REGGIE: Oh yes, oh that auntie, yes.
MR PELHAM: Yes, that auntie. She appears to have given you two black eyes.
REGGIE: Yes, it's a bit sad about her really. She's going a bit doolally. She's convinced she's Joe Bugner.
MR PELHAM: When did Joe Bugner ever give anybody two black eyes?

Regretfully, Mr Pelham feels he has no option but to sack Reggie for being deceitful. Not only has he told him a pack of lies regarding his auntie, but the pig farmer has also discovered Reggie's true identity and bizarre background.

On the same day, Elizabeth also receives her marching orders for typing a letter to a client agreeing with his complaint regarding soggy sponges.

> *Dear Sir,*
> *Thank you for your complaint about our soggy sponges, it makes the eleventh this week. The explanation is simple: frankly, our sponges are soggy. The fault lies in your customers buying overpriced, oversweet, unhealthy, synthetic rubbish.*

Back at home, the unemployed duo decide they must work together in their next endeavour. Elizabeth suggests opening a shop and making their own products to sell, which plants the seed for the primary motivation behind the second series: the founding of the Grot empire.

Elizabeth's idea comes to fruition after Reggie meets up with Jimmy, who is venturing on yet another of his wacky ideas.

(The doorbell rings at Reggie's home. It is Jimmy.)

JIMMY: I know things are awkward; I wouldn't ask normally, but . . .

ELIZABETH: We've got some scrag end of lamb.

JIMMY: Scrag end, toppo. Bit of veg, if it's going? Odd sprout, cheese, butter, bacon, eggs . . . fact is, bit of a cock-up on the catering front.

(Elizabeth goes to the kitchen. Jimmy beckons Reggie to the settee.)

JIMMY: Didn't really come for food – decoy, get big sister out of the way. Got a job for you, interested?

REGGIE: What sort of job, Jimmy?

JIMMY: Can't tell you, hush-hush.

REGGIE: Well I can't very well take a job,

Michael Bilton

Character: Wine buyer, customer in Grot shop.
Series 2, Episode 4.
Born: Yorkshire.
Credits include: TV – *Waiting for God, To the Manor Born* (Ned the gardener).
Update: Worked consistently until his death.
P.S. Played the gardener in the popular *Yellow Pages* ad.

Jimmy, unless I know what it is.

JIMMY: Not time or place; I'll meet you Thursday week.

REGGIE: Right, where?

JIMMY: Can't tell you, classified.

REGGIE: It's going to be a bit difficult to find you, Jimmy, if I don't know where to go.

JIMMY: Good point. My bedsitter 1200 hours, Thursday week – chap I want you to meet.

REGGIE: Really, who . . . I know, it's a secret.

JIMMY: And don't breathe a word to Elizabeth.

REGGIE: There aren't many words I could breathe!

Reggie says that as this is all a decoy there will not be any need for Jimmy to take all the food. But Jimmy says he had better because he does not want Elizabeth thinking she has wasted her time.

When they meet Reggie is not at all interested in Jimmy's plans to form a private army and tells him it is all rubbish - and then stops to think. He's got it! Reggie now realises what they will sell in their

shop: rubbish! He also knows he will call the shop Grot and rushes home to tell Elizabeth, convincing her they will make a fortune and it will be fun.

'I REMEMBER . . I enjoyed working with Len. I was very fond of him and we got on well. But he didn't suffer fools gladly which meant he wasn't universally liked. On recording days he'd start off the morning relaxed and jokey, but you always knew that by about four in the afternoon someone was going to get it - and usually it was some poor sod in the production team.

'But he had the weight of the series resting on his shoulders and it was the fear that within a few hours we'd be filming in front of a live audience that got to him.'

(Bruce Bould)

Glynn Edwards

Character: Mr Pelham, piggery proprietor.
Series 2, Episodes 2, 3, Series 3, Episode 3.
Born: Malaya.
Early career: Sugar farmer in Trinidad.
Credits include: TV – *Minder* (Dave), *Z Cars, Dixon of Dock Green.*
Film – *Rising Damp* (the movie), *The Ipcress File, Zulu.*
Update: Semi-retired, divides time between Spain and houseboat on Thames.
P.S. Often cast as policeman.

Bruce Bould as David Harris-Jones with Prue

Trevor Adams

TONY WEBSTER

The only person Tony Webster fooled with his 'jack the lad' image was himself; everyone else saw him for what he was: a buffoon. One of his qualities was his skill in talking utter drivel, selected from a narrow repertoire of meaningless, kiddish phrases, including: 'success city Arizona', 'knockout!', 'dramatic happening in jelly city' and 'cards-on-the-table-city'. As C.J. said: '. . . the older he gets, the younger he talks.'

Tony worked for Reggie at Sunshine Desserts and Grot with the roles being reversed briefly in between when Reggie, disguised as Martin Wellbourne, reports to Tony. At the commune, Webster is back on Reggie's payroll as culture officer. By this time he has made amends with Joan Greengross, Reggie's former secretary, whom he had earlier married and separated from after straying on his honeymoon with a Finnish 'chick'.

Tony's no longer on the scene so will be missing from the fourth series, having left Joan and headed for a life in New Zealand.

Playing Tony 'he's the kiddie' Webster nearly caused the break-up of Trevor Adams' engagement. 'I was walking down the road with my ex-wife, who I was engaged to at the time, when this woman came rushing up to me. She obviously recognised me from the series, and asked:

"Were you great or were you super?" My ex-wife took it the wrong way and wondered for a while whether I'd enjoyed a night of passion with the woman,' laughs Trevor.

When offered the part of Tony, Trevor headed straight for the library and a copy of David Nobbs's novel. 'I wanted to read the book to get to know the character, but also to see what sort of wordage I was likely to end up with.'

From the very beginning Trevor was proud to be involved with the series. 'It was a great cast and an excellent script. On the surface, Tony was a shallow idiot,' he says, 'but however idiotic people appear in public there's usually a great deal going on behind the facade. It was probably the same with Tony, but within the confines of TV sitcom there wasn't time to explore that side of his character too deeply; and it wasn't particularly appropriate because Tony wasn't the reason for the story.'

Trevor believes one of the beauties of Reggie Perrin was that every character, however minor, had much to offer. 'Everyone had a purpose, even if it was only working as a foil for Leonard, sparking off a different reaction from him. To Joan, his secretary, Reggie revealed a sexual repressive manner, whereas to Tony and David Harris-Jones he played the superiority game, perhaps as a way of getting back at his own inferiority towards C.J.'

While Bruce Bould, playing the slimy but gentle David Harris-Jones, constantly spouted 'Super!', Tony's pet phrase was 'Great!' 'I never thought I'd become involved with a series that used catchphrases, but then Reggie Perrin came along.'

There were many reasons for the series' success, including the exploitation of the catchphrases employed, but Trevor also believes the story had been crying out for years to be written. 'So many people sympathized instantly with how Reggie felt – and still do because life doesn't change.'

Trevor Adams as Tony Webster (far right), who is Reggie's culture officer at the commune

Although he enjoyed the series, Trevor was not particularly sad when the third series finished. 'If the public take to a series like they did with Reggie there's an understandable desire to go on and on; luckily everyone involved with Reggie had enough sense not to try it and I feel they made the right decision.'

The end of the series also marked a significant shift in Trevor's life. In 1982, disillusioned with being a jobbing actor, he began a 12-year excursion into law. 'As far as my TV career was concerned, I felt like the king of one-offs, breezing in and out of character roles,' he says.

'I had the odd meatier role, and did classic shows like *Fawlty Towers*, which was terrific, but began losing job satisfaction; I wanted to do something worthwhile and knowing lawyers employed 'resting' actors to do what is known as sitting behind counsel on behalf of solicitors, I decided to give it a try.'

Trevor was so successful he was offered a permanent job. After deliberating for some time he quit acting for law.

'Initially, I helped barristers maintain all the paper work involved in a case, and liaised on their behalf with the client and their family. Eventually I found myself conducting my own very heavy caseload in several London practices. I was offered a job in Norwich which was ideal because it offered a terrific environment for my daughters to grow up in.'

Now, after more than a decade away from acting, Trevor has returned to the thespian life because he began missing the stage and disliked office politics. Unfortunately he returned too late to be recruited for the new series, and will be a face sadly missing. When David Nobbs wrote *The Legacy of Reginald Perrin* he thought Trevor was still working in law so omitted the character from the new book, sending him off to New Zealand.

But Trevor is keen to resurrect his career, a profession he wanted to follow since his early years growing up in London. 'My first appearance was at the age of three playing a cotton-wool bearded Dopey in *Snow White and the Seven Dwarfs* at Islington's town hall. From there I progressed to school plays, loving every minute.'

After gaining science-based A-levels it seemed Trevor was destined to study medicine, until in 1962, he was fortunate enough to be offered a place in the National Youth Theatre of Great Britain. It changed his life forever. 'I stayed with the youth theatre until I was 21 and then auditioned for and was accepted by RADA.'

After graduating Trevor was desperate for work because he had just got married on the promise of a six-month contract at the Royal Court Theatre, which had fallen through. He was anxious to earn his Equity card so contacted a director he knew who was working on the long-running police series *Z Cars*. 'He kindly offered me a one-line part of a car thief which was enough to get my card.'

By this time prospects looked rosier for Trevor and he moved quickly on to a one-year contract at Stratford-upon-Avon.

The early part of his career was dominated by police series. 'In those days I played all the tearaways on TV, including a villain in *Dixon of Dock Green* and *Softly Softly*. Later, I went on to play all the good guys in the *New Avengers*, *The Professionals*, etc.'

After Reggie Perrin, Trevor appeared on stage in a couple of productions until deciding to switch careers. Now he is back in the business. 'I'm no longer married and my two children have grown up and left home, so I have no responsibilities other than looking after myself – an ideal time to try and resume my acting career.'

EPISODE FOUR:

Reggie and Elizabeth both sacked. Reggie decides to open rather unusual shop.

"Twenty-two minutes late, black ice at Norbiton." (Reggie)

"I didn't get where I am today without knowing Grot would be a success." (C.J.)

"It's the early bird that catches the quick brown fox." (C.J.)

Seeking a loan from C.J., Reggie visits Sunshine Desserts. To his surprise, his former boss agrees on loaning him £30K to help finance his new company, Grot. Sadly, C.J. has not shed his mean, ogre-like image: he believes Reggie has found out about Elizabeth's weekend visit to his Godalming home, is suspecting them of having an affair, and is out to blackmail him.

Del Derrick

Character: Well-dressed man, Grot customer.
Series 2, Episode 4.
Born: London.
Credits include: TV – Secret Army, Variety with Les Dawson, Morecambe & Wise, Bob Monkhouse.
Update: Retired due to ill health.
P.S. Returned from Nairobi to appear in one episode.

Cynthia Etherington

Character: Housewife, Grot customer.
Series 2, Episode 4.
Born: London.
Training: Guild Hall School of Music and Drama.
Credits include: TV – Compact (debut), Z Cars, All Creatures Great and Small.
Update: Retired.

Great empires have to begin somewhere and Grot kicks off in an unassuming little high street shop stating that everything sold in the shop is guaranteed absolutely rubbish. Reggie believes so much rubbish is sold nowadays under false pretences that he thought it would be best being honest about it, hence packing his shelves with square hoops, square footballs, Tom's revolting wine, silent LPs, Dr Snurd's paintings of the Algarve, etc.

First day of trading is slow so Elizabeth – worried no one will ever visit – goes home to bake more tasteless puddings and to make more square hoops.

The first customer is unimpressed with Reggie's new trading concept.

REGGIE: Good morning. Can I help you, madam?
CUSTOMER: Just looking.
REGGIE: Yes, certainly. Give your eyes a feast. Give your optics a treat of a lifetime.
CUSTOMER: It's all rubbish!
REGGIE: Yes, absolutely, complete and utter rubbish.

CUSTOMER: It's stupid!
REGGIE: Thank you very much, I'm very grateful. This is the first of my shops. We hope to have a string stretching from Inverness as far as Penza . . .
(The customer walks out.)

But business picks up and by closing time takings have reached the dizzy heights of £93.82. One customer bought some of Tom's sprout and turnip wine (the worse the taste, the higher the price) for the sister-in-law he hates; another buys a Dr Snurd painting for £40.05 while one chooses a square hoop.

Sales soar and Reggie's single shop

Reggie is unusually bouyant as he leaves for work

Beatrice Shaw

Character: Elderly Grot customer.
Series 2, Episode 4.
Update: Deceased.

quickly turns into Perrin Products (Grot) Ltd., based at Perrin House. In two years he has opened 44 shops and company profits stand at £750,000. His fortunes have lifted him back into the realms of social acceptability within the neighbourhood and the likes of Dennis Milford and two-faced Peter Cartwright are throwing out invitations to dinner like confetti – all of which Reggie smugly declines.

For what turns out to be a brief moment in his life, Reggie is excited and interested in his work, and during the morning ritual he actually tells Elizabeth he will have a good time at the office.

But life can never be perfect, and the sole blemish for Reggie is his new secretary: the extremely staid, serious and poker-faced Miss Erith. Reggie decides he will try to get Joan back.

Gilly Flower

Character: Woman with fur, Grot customer.
Series 2, Episode 4.
Born: London.
Credits include: TV – Fawlty Towers (Miss Tibbs).
Update: Retired in 1991, aged 81. P.S. Gave up acting to work in personnel for six years.

Edward Dentith

Character: Dennis Milford, Reggie's neighbour.
Series 2, Episode 4.
Born: Birmingham.
Credits include: TV – Emmerdale Farm. Film – Sea Wolves.
Theatre – Dial M For Murder.

Reggie's planning meeting brings back two familiar faces from the first series: Morris Coates from the advertising agency and Esther Pigeon from Market Research. With Reggie and David Harris-Jones, who is now working at Grot, they discuss the new product ideas, including: a new silent LP, 'Laryngitis in 30 Lands', featuring the

Joan Blackham

Character: Miss Erith, secretary, Perrin Products.
Series 2, Episodes 4, 5.
Born: Wolverhampton.
Early career: Secretary.
Credits include: TV – To the Manor Born, Dangerfield, Inspector Morse.
Update: Does supply teaching when not acting.

silence of Max Bygraves, Des O'Connor, Bay City Rollers, Sex Pistols and Rolf Harris; upright models of Pisa; rubber razor blades for nervous shavers; porous waterbeds; mousetraps made entirely of cheese and the ideal gift for the motorist you do not like: the elastic towrope.

Later that week, Reggie visits Sunshine Desserts. While he is there, he discovers where Joan is working from Tony Webster and repays the £30K loan to C.J. As he leaves the building, newspaper headlines catch his eye: 'Food firm crumble – Jelly giant bankrupt.' Reggie laughs.

'I REMEMBER . . . I always talked in percentages, and before filming my scene Gareth would say: "And good luck, Jacki!"

'It was certainly a testing part and his good luck wish made me more nervous of fluffing it up, especially as it was recorded in front of a live audience. There was a slight blip in this episode when I knew I hadn't quite got it right, not that anyone would have noticed, but I knew I just had to soldier on.' *(Jacki Piper)*

EPISODE FIVE:

Reggie's rubbish shops Grot are an amazing success. Sunshine Desserts bankrupt.

"Twenty-two minutes late, fractured . . . doesn't matter!"   (Reggie)

**"I didn't get where you are today without knowing the night is darkest before the storm."
(C.J.)**

While Reggie opens his 50th shop, C.J. goes on the dole. After suffering 25 years under C.J.'s thumb Reggie decides it is time to get his own back - perhaps he will offer him a job. He also plans offering Joan a job. Even Elizabeth is offered a job by Reggie with a starting date of June 1st, but not until she threatened him with not getting any dinner.

From Perrin House, Reggie telephones C.J. at Blancmange Tower, and enjoys dishing out a dose of his own medicine.

REGGIE: C.J.? Perrin here, Reggie Perrin, on red. C.J., . . . what? Oh thank you, yes, 50 shops now. Sorry to hear of your troubles. (Reggie holds the phone away and laughs.) There's a vague possibility that I might be able to offer you a job, C.J. When will it be convenient for you to come and see me? Tuesday the 1st at 10, fine, make it Friday the 4th at 3. Goodbye!

When C.J. arrives for his interview, Reggie exploits the role reversals to the full.

(C.J. knocks)
REGGIE: 1-2-3-4 make him sweat outside the door; 5-6-7-8 always pays to make them wait; 9-10 come!

Ah, C.J., come in, come in, good to see you. Do sit down, C.J.

C.J.: Thank you, Reggie.

(The chair blows off.)

REGGIE: (Laughing) That damn new chair, most embarrassing, C.J. The perils of buying British.

C.J.: Absolutely, yes.

REGGIE: Cigar, C.J.? Help yourself.

C.J.: Thank you, Reggie. (Chair blows off)

REGGIE: Lighter? Ashtray, C.J?

(The chair blows off again.)

REGGIE: Well, we meet in altered circumstances, C.J.

C.J.: We do indeed.

REGGIE: The slings and arrows of outrageous fortune.

C.J.: I couldn't have put it better myself.

REGGIE: The night is darkest before the storm.

C.J.: Precisely, I didn't get where you are today without knowing the night is darkest before the storm.

REGGIE: Now, C.J. Tell me. Do you think you can work happily with me as your boss?

C.J.: Reggie, you asked me a straight question, I'm going to give you a straight answer. I've always taken great pains not to talk in clichés. Mrs C.J. and I have always avoided clichés like the plague. A cliché to me is like a red rag to a bull. However, there is the exception that proves the rule and there is a cliché that fits my situation like a glove.

Reggie: And that is?

C.J.: Necessity is the mother of intention. In other words, Reggie, I am forced to consider working for you.

Reggie offers C.J. a job working on EuroGrot, the company's arm in Europe. He also asks him to start on June 1st.

Next, Reggie interviews Tony Webster.

REGGIE: Ah, Tony, Tony; do come in, do come in; do sit down, do sit down.

TONY: Thanks.

REGGIE: I was awfully sorry to hear about Sunshine Desserts.

TONY: Dramatic happenings in jelly city, sensations in triflesville.

(Reggie offers Tony a cigar.)

TONY: No, thanks, Reggie, health city!

REGGIE: And what are you planning to do next?

TONY: Well, I've had lots of fantastic offers. Don't know which one to take.

REGGIE: So my offer of a job is rather pointless?

TONY: Well, look, this is cards-on-the-table city; in the long-term, in the long-term Tony Webster's still the lad. He's the kiddie.

REGGIE: Absolutely, but in the short-term?

TONY: Nothing.

REGGIE: I can offer you a job starting on . . . shall we say,

Reggie and Elizabeth enjoy a rare moment of contentment

June 1st?
Tony: Great!

The 1st of June arrives and Reggie and Elizabeth head off to work together for the

first time. Reggie tells Elizabeth she has got a nice assistant working for her – little does she know it is C.J.

To everyone's horror, all the new recruits (or old crowd) arrive together in Reggie's

office, unaware that they would be working together again. Just another of Reggie's surprises.

When Reggie tells Joan that employing her and Tony at Grot was partly in the hope that they would reconcile their marital differences, they devise a plan to try to make Tony jealous.

Various ploys fail so Joan suggests visiting Reggie's home while Elizabeth is away in Holland. Weak-willed Reggie finally crumbles and the stage is set for history to repeat itself - and it nearly does. During the evening, it is not long before Joan pulls Reggie upstairs to the spare bedroom again, but then the doorbell rings just like last time. Once again Joan has to negotiate the drainpipe to make her escape. But the scheme fails: it does nothing to incite jealousy in Tony.

Next, Reggie visits Joan's home but when Tony arrives Reggie has the pleasure of escaping via Joan's drainpipe. The problem is that it is two storeys up. But it is all worth it because the plan works and Joan and Tony reunite.

Reggie's contentment and happiness with life are short-lived when one evening he starts blurting out phrases normally associated with C.J.

REGGIE: I just used one of C.J.'s phrases, I'm not getting to be like him, am I?
ELIZABETH: No, Reggie, of course you're not.
REGGIE: God, I didn't get where I am today without getting to be like . . . I've done it again, oh my God!
ELIZABETH: Now Reggie, don't sigh. You're supposed to be happy.
REGGIE: Yes, I am aren't I? What does my happiness mean, darling? What does my success add up to? Every morning, I get up, get dressed, go downstairs, have breakfast, leave the house, go down Coleridge Close, turn right into Tennyson Avenue, right into

Wordsworth Drive, catch the train, arrive 22 minutes late, walk to Perrin products, go in, dictate letters, hold conferences, make decisions, have lunch, make decisions, hold conferences, dictate letters, leave, catch the train to Climthorpe, arrive 22 minutes late, walk up Coleridge Close, right into Tennyson Avenue, left into Wordsworth Drive, go into the house I left that morning, have supper, go up the stairs I came down that morning, take off the clothes I put on that morning, clean the teeth I cleaned that morning and get into the bed that I got out of that morning.'

Elizabeth is worried Reggie is going to start acting strange again, but he puts her mind at ease by telling her that he is simply tired. But he is much more than tired: by spelling out the structure of his day Reggie has shown to himself that life has in many ways turned full circle. Once he tried desperately to break the routine and monotony of his everyday life in search of new values and freedom. Now he finds himself stuck back in just another rut, albeit cloaked in a different identity: Grot instead of Sunshine Desserts. Perhaps it is time to do something about it again?

'I REMEMBER. . . I'd been in the business three years when I landed the part of Miss Erith. Just before it I'd filmed an American Express advert playing a car hire girl. Leonard had been filming one of the Martini adverts at the same studios and had seen me. He suggested to Gareth – who I'd already worked for in *To the Manor Born* – that I play the secretary, and I was offered the part.

'I was working in theatre at Chichester at the time, so caught the 5 p.m. London train for evening rehearsals. It was a very exciting time.'

(Joan Blackham)

Bruce Bould

DAVID HARRIS-JONES

David Harris-Jones was the sort of chap you either felt sorry for and agreed needed a little mothering, or drove you to despair with his constant stuttering, attenuated sentences, wimpish attitudes and irritating mannerisms.

Greasy-haired David, who was always spouting 'super!', was educated at a minor public school. He was a body of adjectives: shy, hardworking, honest, dutiful, as well as being ineffective, diffident and someone who, try as he might, will never progress beyond the ranks of junior management.

At Sunshine Desserts, David worked in sales and reported to Reggie. After being made redundant by C.J. just before his wedding, he was taken under Reggie's wing and became Grot's Head of Expansion (U.K.). Later, after leaving his job at a building society, David joined the commune as the sex therapist – not the job for the world's shyest stutterer. When the community collapsed, David – together with wife Prue, their matching jumpers and son, Reggie, named after his godfather – returned to the family firm in Haverfordwest, where David worked in the communications department. Sadly, after the firm was taken over by a conglomerate, history repeated itself and David was dumped on the dole.

In the fourth series, David has reached 50 and is still married to Prue. Their son

has become something of an embarrassment. After leaving school at 15, Reggie ran away at 16, got a gypsy pregnant at 17, and now lives in a lay-by on the A18.

When Bruce Bould was first offered the part of David Harris-Jones, he turned it down.

'I'd just finished a West End play with Alec Guinness when John Howard Davies – who went on to direct the Reggie Perrin pilot – cast me as a hippy in an episode of *The Good Life*. It was my first sitcom and went very well,' says Bruce.

'Then my agent called to say John wanted me to play a small part in *The Fall and Rise of Reginald Perrin.* I turned it down unread because I'd just finished a nice part in *The Good Life* and wanted more than I thought the part of David could offer.'

Two days later the phone rang again. 'It was John Howard Davies, who said: "I think you're making a big mistake, Bruce – go and read the book." So I nipped down the local library, borrowed a copy and found it extremely funny.'

It did not take long for Bruce to realise that if the show went beyond the pilot the role of David Harris-Jones would blossom significantly. 'Even then I only reluctantly agreed to play the part. The pilot quickly led to the commissioning of series one which was a joy to work on.'

In many ways, David presented Bruce

**Bruce Bould and Theresa Watson as David
and Prue Harris-Jones in Series Four**

Bould with quite a challenge. With the
character's perpetual stuttering and
constant fawning, he was probably one of
the most difficult characters to play.

'When I first received the scripts, I didn't
know how to play it. There's a line in the
original book describing David as "walking
with a stutter". So as well as in his talk, I
tried to capture that in the walk and his
overall appearance. The first thing I decided
was that the character should have lank,
unkempt hair.'

When it came to selecting the apposite
suit for David Harris-Jones, Bruce knew

just what he wanted. 'The BBC Wardrobe
Department thought I was a bit odd
because I told them I wanted a suit that
looked awful and at least a size too big.'

Bruce was successful in lifting his
character from the printed page and
creating the hilarious David who stuttered
his way through a multitude of scenes in
the first series.

In the second and third, Bruce began to
notice a significant increase in hesitations
in the script. 'I had to be careful not to let
the hesitations dominate too much and to
retain other characteristics, like the
portrayal of a man desperately trying to do
the right thing.

The fourth series reveals a subtle
reduction in the amount of stutters David
has to endure, an indication, perhaps, that

he has gained a little self-confidence in the two decades since the commune's demise.

'He's also older which naturally makes a big difference,' says Bruce, who was a little sceptical when plans for the new series were first mooted. 'I remember saying to myself: "My God, I don't know about this. Twenty years later and without the main character - it's like *Blake's Seven* without Blake!" But, of course, it all depends on the quality of the writing.'

Once again Bruce read the book and quickly realised that in *The Legacy of Reginald Perrin*, David Nobbs had come up with another gem. 'What David's done is succeed in highlighting a new social angst: ageism and early redundancy. And he's been clever in replacing a powerful male character, which was Reggie, with a powerful female character, Geraldine Hackstraw, the solicitor.'

There is no doubting the fun Bruce has had resurrecting a character that has lived with him for so long. 'David Harris-Jones has always been marvellous to play. He's a sympathetic character but infuriating, which is nice.'

Bruce believes one reason the original three series were so successful was their phenomenal pace, generated largely by Leonard Rossiter. 'His speed of delivery rubbed off on the rest of us, and eventually filming sped along so fast you didn't have to think about it.'

Born in Bradford, Bruce remembers wanting to act since the age of ten. 'What started the ball rolling was starring as Toad in Toad of Toad Hall at Bradford's Civic Playhouse in a children's amateur production. My parents were both amateur actors so I guess it was in the blood.'

Aged 17, Bruce was invited to the Birmingham Rep as acting ASM. He had just finished a year of his A-levels when offered the opportunity. 'I only stayed four months because I got into RADA, but it was great experience.'

Bruce was fortunate enough to know that upon graduating from drama school he had a job waiting for him. 'My boss had assured me there was a place for me back at Birmingham, however bad I was,' laughs Bruce, 'so I returned in 1969 and did another three years.'

While at the rep, Bruce met Theresa Watson, who became his wife in 1972, and screen wife, Prue, a few years later in Reggie Perrin.

By the mid 70s, Bruce had already played several small parts in various TV productions, including *New Scotland Yard*, but his debut – as it seems with most of the acting profession – was in *Z Cars*. His first leading part was in an episode of the BBC's ill-fated *Churchill's People* in 1975.

Then after two successful plays, *Clever Soldiers* at the Hampstead Theatre Club, and six months in *A Family and a Fortune*, at London's Apollo Theatre – with Alec Guinness and Margaret Leighton – came the part of Guy, the hero-worshipping student in *The Good Life*, who was besotted with Tom Good's life of self-sufficiency.

Since Reggie Perrin – which he classes as the highlight of his TV career – Bruce has been seen in *To the Manor Born, Shelley, Drop the Dead Donkey, Shine on Harvey Moon, Strangers,* etc. His last major TV appearance was in three series of *Howard's Way*, while his last stage role was in 1990, playing John Worthing in *The Importance of Being Earnest* at Windsor.

Without a doubt, Bruce's TV career has been dominated by comedy. 'I like playing comedy. I found for a while after the earlier series of Reggie Perrin I was constantly being asked to play berks, which I hated in some ways. I always made sure I played the other roles differently from the way I played David because to me he wasn't a berk.'

EPISODE SIX:

More and more success for Grot. Reggie now employing C.J., Elizabeth, Joan, Tony and David.

"I didn't get where I am today without recognising a completely useless machine when I see one." (C.J.)

Before heading off to work, Reggie tells his cat, Ponsonby, about the uncontrollable monster called Grot he has created. After setting it up as a final defiant gesture to the world, success escalated out of control. Now, Reggie is tired of being a tycoon and has decided to destroy the company by employing people in jobs for which they are totally unsuitable.

The first appointment is Doc Morrisey, who by now has been struck off the medical register for gross professional

incompetence. He is recruited as Head of Forward Planning.

The next recruit is Seamus Finnegan, an Irish labourer working on the Climthorpe slip relief, Feeder Road: an ideal choice in Reggie's eyes for the administration officer's role.

During a short break on the south coast with Elizabeth, Tom, Linda and their two kids, Reggie persuades Tom to join him at Grot as Head of Publicity by flattering him on his qualities – for which the gormless idiot falls.

Soon Jimmy is added to the list of new employees after he is taken for yet another ride by one of his supposed 'top drawer' friends. This time it is Clive 'Lofty' Anstruther who does a runner with money and equipment while Jimmy was planning to set up a secret army. Jimmy is offered the prestigious role of Grot's Head of Creative Thinking.

Heading the boardroom table at Perrin House, Reggie asks his new recruits to supply a resumé of their current progress. Tom has been asked to start things off, during which his confidence as a publicity person grows considerably.

TOM: I had distributed among you a few campaign ideas. I'm not really a campaign person. And slogans, I won't bore you with my slogan ideas now.
REGGIE: No, no, Tom. I insist you bore us with them now.
TOM: Well, there was one. I'm not really a slogan person, it, um, was: 'Go to Grot shops and get an eye full of Perrins products with a wide range of goods that are really pretty awful.'
REGGIE: Excellent, Tom.
TOM: It doesn't rhyme or scan properly.
REGGIE: It almost rhymes and scans properly, that's the important thing. This is exactly the thing I'm paying you for.

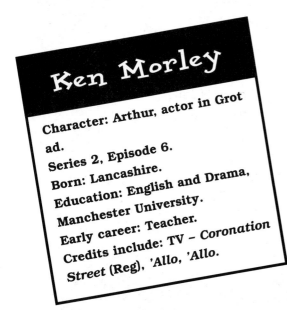

Ken Morley

Character: Arthur, actor in Grot ad.
Series 2, Episode 6.
Born: Lancashire.
Education: English and Drama, Manchester University.
Early career: Teacher.
Credits include: TV – Coronation Street (Reg), 'Allo, 'Allo.

Sheila Bernette

Character: Gladys, actress in Grot ad alongside Ken Morley's Arthur.
Series 2, Episode 6.
Born: London.
Training: Italia Conti.
Credits include: TV – The Black and White Minstrel Show, The Saturday Crowd, The Tommy Cooper Show.
Update: Appears regularly at the Players Theatre.
P.S. Sheila and Ken filmed a similar advert promoting Sharp's Extra Strong mints in the 70s.

Derry Power

Character: Seamus Finnegan, Grot's admin officer.
Series 2, Episode 6.
Series 3, Episode 6.

TOM: Well, thank you. I'll give you one more perhaps. 'Grot is the ideal place for gifts because it's all on one floor and there aren't any lifts.'
(Everyone claps.)
TOM: They aren't all of that standard, of course.

Doc Morrisey introduces his idea of January sales in September with fantastic price increases instead of everything being slashed, while Jimmy shows a machine he has made which is completely useless – which could well be another bestseller in the shops.

Reggie becomes decidedly more depressed when his plan to destroy Grot backfires and Tom's slogans become famous, Jimmy's useless machine cannot be made quick enough to meet demand and Seamus's work flows help save the company thousands of pounds.

The next step for Reggie to stop this runaway success is to sack Doc, Tom, Jimmy and Seamus, but he finds it impossible for a whole list of reasons. So he confides in Joan that to destroy Grot he will have to start behaving eccentrically again - something he seems to have done all his life.

'I REMEMBER . . . that for filming the holiday scenes we wanted bad weather and got it with rain and wind. Just in case, we had the fire brigade on standby to produce rain and even a wind machine which, luckily, we didn't need because it was horrendous conditions: cold, wet and windy. We were desperately trying to hide from the holidaymakers how happy we were about the bad weather. I even got a walk-on part in the episode. When Reggie is parked on the sea front I can be seen walking across the car park in the rain.'
(David Nobbs)

EPISODE SEVEN:

Reggie fed up with success of Grot. Tries to destroy it. Result - even more success.

"Twenty-two minutes late, escaped puma, Chessington North." (Reggie)

"I didn't get where I am today without asking for 10p for a cup of tea, guv'." (C.J.)

Reggie's behaviour becomes even more outlandish when he kisses Joan in front of Elizabeth and gives outrageous exclusive interviews to BBC1, BBC2 and ITV on *Pillock Talk*, *The World Tomorrow Today* and *Hi Finance*.

Over the next few days everyone praises Reggie on his wonderful interviews, and it seems whatever he

Timothy Carlton

Character: Colin Pillock, BBC interviewer.
Series 2, Episode 7.
Series 3, Episode 5.
Born: Reading.
Credits include: TV – Family at War, The Liver Birds, The Onedin Line, Ripping Yarns, Don't Wait Up.
Film – The Lucky Touch, In Search of Eden, C.A.T.S. Eyes.

does he can no longer shock the people around him, including C.J. When he asks Reggie for his attention because he has an urgent problem, Reggie agrees and immediately dictates a non-urgent letter to one of the Grot shop managers.

Dear Sir,
I am sorry to hear you have not yet received our supplies of edible furniture; this can only be due to non-arrival of supplies. I am, however, deeply disturbed to hear you have not yet received our new range of dentures for pets which are proving so popular with bloody silly idiots who put little doggy dentures in glasses of water beside their kennels and even littler budgie dentures in even smaller glasses of water beside their cages.
Yours faithfully,
Reginald I. Perrin

When Joan suggests this inability to shock people is probably because they all know him too well, Reggie decides to turn his attention to strangers.

When Mr Herbert – an applicant for the North Eastern Sales Area job – arrives for an interview, Reggie decides it is time to shock a stranger. When he goes to sit down, Reggie pulls the chair from beneath him so he crashes to the floor. He then teases him over his dandruff problem.

REGGIE: You've got to get rid of that dandruff, you realise that?
MR HERBERT: Oh yes, I do have a slight dandruff problem.
REGGIE: Yes, you're in an ongoing dandruff situation. There's a chap in Switzerland cures it in a fortnight.'
MR HERBERT: Oh, really?
REGGIE: Very painful, of course: starvation and electrodes. Stands you upside down, straps you down, passes electric current through you and when the voltage reaches a certain height your hair stands on end and all the dandruff just flies off.
MR HERBERT: Oh, dear. Is it absolutely necessary?
REGGIE: Absolutely necessary, and what about your socks, have you no taste?
MR HERBERT: They're a present from my aunt.
REGGIE: Aunts are one thing, commerce is another, socks are two things.
MR HERBERT: I realise that.
REGGIE: What is your name? Herbert, Hubert, Herbert?
MR HERBERT: Herbert.
REGGIE: Herbert, right. Tell me, Hubert, you don't mind me insulting you like this?
MR HERBERT: You have a reputation for being a bit unusual. I think a genius has a right to be.
REGGIE: Of course I haven't. I haven't got any right at all, Mr Herbert. I do apologise.

David Rowlands

Character: Mr Herbert, job applicant.
Series 2, Episode 7.
Born: Abergavenny.
Training: Guild Hall School of Music & Drama.
Credits include: TV – Dr Who, The Two Ronnies, Rising Damp.
Update: Lives on farm in Wales.
P.S. Has also worked for Radio Sussex as a reporter and is a qualified teacher.

Even if I were a genius I'd have no right to be rude, I'm sorry.

Reggie's attempts to shock have failed again, even with a stranger. He tries another stranger, this time Mr Percy Lisburn. He pretends to be gay but unfortunately this does not shock the Grot shop manager one bit, because he is gay himself.

In one last effort, Reggie visits a local pub wearing a beige wig, dress, padded bra, handbag and glasses. But everybody acknowledges him, unaffected by his weird attire. Realising there is nothing he can ever do now that will shock the world, not even dressing up as a woman, he heads home.

That evening Reggie convinces Elizabeth that possessions are worthless, and that togetherness is the most important feature of life. He persuades her to run off with him and to re-enact his previous faked suicide scenario.

After telling the family that they are off to the Woking flower show but that it might be some time before they see each other again, Reggie and Elizabeth drive to the same Dorset beach and replace their clothes of normality with the disguise of tramps.

The following day, Mr and Mrs Gossamer (a.k.a. Mr and Mrs Perrin) sit contemplating their future when an uncannily familiar tramp walks by scrounging 10p. When he replies: 'I didn't get where I am today without asking for 10p for a cup of tea, guv,' Reggie wonders whether it could really be C.J.

Reggie and Elizabeth plan their exit

A disguised C.J. points to the cliff and when Reggie and Elizabeth look down onto the beach below they cannot believe their eyes. A string of people stretching for miles are all taking the Perrins' example by undressing and leaving their old identity behind on the beach in search of a better life.

But life's frustrations and routines cannot

Character: Mr Lisburn, manager, Grot, W1.
Series 2, Episode 7.
Born: Liverpool.
Early career: Fencing instructor at LAMDA.
Credits include: TV – *The Beiderbecke Affair*, *The Beiderbecke Tapes*, *Andy Capp*, *Last of the Summer Wine*.
P.S. Taught Donald Sutherland at LAMDA.

Blain Fairman

Character: Sheridan Honeydew, interviewer,
Series 2, Episode 7.
Born: Canada.
Credits include: Film – The Trap.
Update: Now partner in a London conference and production company.
P.S. Has written and produced for the BBC.

Gareth Gwenlan, producer of the show

be shrugged off or discarded by a simple change of clothes, as Reggie and Elizabeth will soon discover again as they walk away into the distance.

'I REMEMBER . . . the final scene of the episode where Reggie and Elizabeth walk away from the cliff edge was filmed from a helicopter. It was about 5 a.m. when this helicopter swooped down to pick the camera team and me up. We mounted the camera and took off. We had arranged with Len and Pauline that the cue to turn and walk away would come from me with a great flash of the torch.

'We'd just lined up the shot when this guy walks into view with his dog and decides to stop and watch. I couldn't make Len see because the man was behind, so I asked the pilot to land which he did by placing one ski on the cliff edge. I got the matter sorted out but no sooner had I stepped back into the helicopter than the pilot tipped the machine and flew off - I was not impressed.

'In the end, we got the shot completed. A week later, I heard the pilot had killed himself by crashing into the Thames after missing a landing platform.'

(Gareth Gwenlan)

Neville Barber

Character: Peregrine Trembleby, interviewer, Hi Finance.
Series 2, Episode 7.
Born: Manchester.
Training: RADA.
Early career: Teacher.
Credits include: TV – Chronicle, Dr Who, Upstairs, Downstairs, General Hospital, Les Dawson Show, Churchill's People.
Update: Lives in Scotland and works in theatre.

Theresa Watson

PRUE HARRIS-JONES

Prue had married David during his days at Grot, but did not appear until the third series. Invited by Reggie and Elizabeth to join Perrins, she was given responsibility for crafts: thatching, basket-weaving, etc.

Prue once told Reggie that the reason her marriage was so strong was because she and David agreed on everything. They were certainly true to their word and even liked the same clothes, often choosing similar colours as well as styles.

The only row to threaten their marriage occurred when Prue spotted David leaving Deborah Swaffham's bedroom (a guest at the commune). Prue misinterpreted the scene and, believing her hubby was having an affair with the sex-craving brunette, left for her mother's in Exeter.

This short-lived separation ended when she returned to help defend Perrins from the thugs who vandalised the commune.

In many ways, Prue was ideally suited to David, and saw her main function in life as supporting her spouse whenever possible. Loyal and dependable, she was the steadying influence and boost of strength David so desperately needed.

Except for the temporary marital hitch at the commune, Prue and David's marriage is solid and it's not surprising that even after 20 years, they are still together in the fourth series

Theresa Watson – wife of actor Bruce Bould – has author David Nobbs to thank for the offer to play David Harris-Jones's devoted wife, Prue.

'I was a Reggie Perrin groupie,' laughs Theresa. 'I saw all 14 episodes of the first two series being recorded and attended every aftershow party, so got to know everyone involved with the programme.'

By the third series David Harris-Jones had got married and the hunt was on for a suitable wife who could appear. 'David Nobbs thought the obvious solution was for me to play Prue. Happily, director Gareth Gwenlan agreed so I was asked and, not surprisingly, accepted.'

When Theresa saw the scripts, she knew she would enjoy playing Prue, though she realised the part was not going to be

Theresa Watson (right) as David Harris-Jones's wife Prue

straightforward. It meant fitting in very precisely with her husband's well-established performance, without becoming a mere shadow.

'At times, David and Prue said things in unison which meant being spot-on with timings. But I had a great time, and particularly enjoyed filming in Cheltenham during a hot summer.

Already knowing everyone meant I didn't encounter difficulties fitting in. The whole atmosphere was similar to that of a happy little repertory company,' explains Theresa, who had worked with Leonard Rossiter twice before on TV.

Enthused by the prospect of joining her husband in the third series, Theresa even got the knitting needles out! 'For some reason, Bruce and I were convinced that David and Prue would wear matching sweaters - so I knitted them.

'The funny thing was that I had finished the sweaters before reading the scripts or David Nobbs's third novel in the series, *The Better World of Reginald Perrin*, and discovering he'd actually put the characters in matching jumpers!'

Playing Prue is one of the highlights of Theresa's TV career. 'The series seems to have been part of my life ever since it first started, nearly two decades ago, what with all the repeats and constant interest.

Although Theresa only appeared in one series compared with Bruce, who was in all three, she was the one stopped in the street by people recognising her from the show.

But then Theresa's had more experience of being recognised by the public: she got used to being stopped in the street during a 24-week stint in *Crossroads*, in which she played Benny's girlfriend, Josie Welch.

'I was accused of leading the gullible Benny astray,' explains Theresa. 'People used to stop me and shout: "You leave that poor Benny alone!" – quite frightening.'

Even though she only appeared in the soap for six months, she made such an impression in the show that kids were knocking at her door asking for an autograph.

Although she was born in Essex, Theresa spent much of her childhood in Kent. Her family's only connection with the stage was through an aunt who attended RADA before the Second World War.

'Her career had only just begun when war broke out. After the war, she took up horticulture. I think my mother would also have liked to become a professional actress, but instead she stuck to amateur dramatics, which she introduced me to while I was still at school.'

Theresa has wanted to act ever since she can remember, and applied to drama school while studying for A-levels. After training, she served an apprenticeship in rep, beginning at Billingham, then Chester, before moving to Birmingham, where she met Bruce.

After writing to the director, Theresa made her TV debut in *The Girl* on the M1, and her sole film appearance – playing Gladys in the Bryan Forbes movie, *The Raging Moon* – followed shortly after.

Other TV credits include: Grace (a prison officer) in Granada's *Lady Killers*; Abigail in *Within These Walls*; Mrs Cranley in *Don't Wait Up*; Henrietta in *Clayhanger*; and Dorothy (a lab assistant) in *Grange Hill*.

Her theatrical credits include numerous spells at The National Theatre in productions such as *Saint Joan, The Women* and *Mandragola*.

Theresa's career spans all media, but she has a preference for the stage. 'In the theatre you're always playing to a live audience which generates a unique excitement not found elsewhere, except, perhaps, in front of an invited audience for a sitcom.'

SERIES THREE:

The Commune – 'In Search of a Better Life'

EPISODE ONE:

"I didn't get where I am today by being nice!" (C.J.)

"Absence is better than a cure." (C.J.)

Reggie and Elizabeth walking the countryside as Mr and Mrs Gossamer seem pleased with their newly-found freedom, until resting on a bank they realise they are not truly content.

Deciding to revert to their previous identities, Reggie suggests selling Grot and their home and when they are rich they will really be free of life's burdens. To celebrate they decide to have a drink. While sipping champagne on a hotel terrace, Elizabeth comments on Reggie's constant sighing.

ELIZABETH: If you're so happy, Reggie, why do you keep sighing?
REGGIE: Well, sheer bliss isn't enough, is it?
ELIZABETH: Oh, Reggie.
REGGIE: There must be something more for me to do than sit by the sea guzzling champagne.

ELIZABETH: Oh, Reggie, will you never be content?
REGGIE: I'm just an ordinary bloke you know. I'm no different from anyone else who walked out on his job, faked suicide, started a new life, returned in disguise, remarried his wife, opened up a shop selling things guaranteed absolutely useless, amazingly succeeded, walked out again, faked another suicide and started another new life.
ELIZABETH: But no one else has done that.
REGGIE: Exactly, darling, so there must be some purpose behind it. No, there's something I've got to do, darling. A plan to

Brian Coburn

Character: Big man in bank.
Series 3, Episode 1.
Born: Scotland.
Credits include: TV – *God's Wonderful Railway.*
Film – *Carry On Dick, Octopussy.*
Update: Died in 1989, aged 53.
P.S. Made over 200 TV appearances.

help fight the miseries of this poor ol' world. A brilliant idea that will make everything I've done so far seem a mere bagatelle. A plan that will send the name of Perrin ringing out proudly for posterity.
ELIZABETH: Darling, what plan?

Ali Baba

Character: Man in park.
Series 3, Episode 1.
Born: Pakistan.
Credits include: TV – EastEnders.
Update: Full-time magician

An altercation in the bank gives Reggie a brainwave

REGGIE: I wish I knew. I expect I'll think of something.

The idea for his next project comes to him when he encounters a row that nearly comes to blows between two men in a bank over a trivial matter. Reggie has a brainwave that sets him up for the third series: establishing a community for the middle-aged and middle class where people can learn to live in love and happiness.

Elizabeth gives her wholehearted support to the idea and while she takes responsibility for furnishing the house in Botchley, Reggie decides to find the staff. Top of his list is C.J. whom he finds busking outside a cinema dressed as a tramp. Over a drink he offers him a job with a £10K salary, free board and lodgings – although this will be under canvas.

Next, he hunts Doc Morrisey, and finds him feeding starlings in a park. Working – just about – as an English teacher with the adopted title Professor, Doc Morrisey confesses to having just one student. Within minutes the Doc has agreed to become the commune's psychologist.

Tony Webster, who has also been struggling since the days of Grot, takes little persuasion.

TONY: A community, that is a great idea, REGGIE. Knockout!

REGGIE: What a pity your export/import business is doing so well.

TONY: It is, it is, yes. Tony Webster's still the kiddie. I'm off to Frankfurt, tonight. Yes, hit the Fatherlands, score a few exports. This is success city Arizona.

REGGIE: Is it really? So you won't be interested in my little offer of £5K a year, every year.

TONY: Well, ah . . . I'll talk it over with Joanie. After all, she is my wife. (He looks at his watch.) Well, must fly.

REGGIE: Yes, Heathrow calls.

(Tony picks up his briefcase, it opens and brochures fall out.)

REGGIE: Not taking a great deal of luggage with you, more reading matter I see. (He reads a brochure). 'Uniwarm, the only central heating system that doesn't blow draughts in your pocket.'

TONY: Yes, OK. Cards on the tablesville, Arizona. Not going to Frankfurt. Working for the Uniwarm Central Heating . . . All right, no basic, but fantastic commission, knockout! We'll take the job, Reggie.

David and his wife, Prue, are overjoyed to be invited to join Reggie's new community. In their matching fawn cardigans and

David Hanson

Character: Bank clerk.
Series 3, Episode 1.
Credits include: TV – *Rumpole of the Old Bailey, Bread, Strike it Rich, There Comes a Time.*
Update: Lives in Thailand where he teaches English at university.

Leslie Rhodes

Character: Barman.
Series 3, Episode 1.
Born: Romford.
Early career: Accountant.
Credits include: TV – *Second Thoughts.*
Update: Combines occasional acting with life as an accountant.
P.S. Used to be Dick Emery's stand-in.

garish yellow shirts, David and Prue seem ideally suited to one another.

Now Reggie has the unenviable job of telling Elizabeth that all the old cronies are going to work at the commune. It is interesting that when Reggie needs recruits for his latest project, it is the old crowd that he turns to. He seems to need them just as much as they depend on him for employment and an existence. As Reggie says: 'It'll be like having an old pair of pyjamas. A bit torn here and there, but a

George Tovey

Character: *Little man in bank.*
Series 3, Episode 1.
Update: Deceased.

Arnold Peters

Character: *Mr Penfold,*
complaining neighbour.
Series 3, Episode 2.

man feels comfortable having them around him.' Other recruits for the commune include Linda and Tom.

The first day of Perrins, the commune, arrives and all the old familiar faces set up their tents in the back garden before an introductory meeting to find out the purpose of this latest venture. Reggie describes it as a 'cross between a commune and a self-help therapy centre'. People are going to come here, stay as long as they like and pay as much as they like.

Jobs are also dished out. Elizabeth becomes secretary, Doc Morrisey is the psychologist, Tom is responsible for sport,

Joan music, Tony culture, Prue Old English crafts, C.J. work, Linda art and David sex.

'I REMEMBER . . . I loved working with Len. I admired him and I learnt a lot from him.

'Even now when I watch any of the old episodes there always seems something new to learn. His timing and delayed timing were superb, particularly with the gags like when he's drinking Tom's homemade wine: you know what's coming, but he delays his response for a few seconds and then you get his reaction – it's superb. I wish I had the ability to do it myself. Often when we were filming a scene which didn't include me, I had to leave the set because I couldn't stop laughing!'

(Sue Nicholls)

**Reggie holds an
introductory meeting**

EPISODE TWO:

"Cock-up on judgment of men front."
(Jimmy)

"It's drugs with me, man!"
(David Harris-Jones)

Jimmy is recruited as the leader of Grot's expeditionary force when his narrow boats business collapses. Reggie also receives two complaints about the commune.

Mr Penfold from number 21 and Mrs Hollies from number 19 complain about the tents, bugles, cars, all the people, the music and babies crying. Reggie tells them that this is just the beginning: soon there will be

Reggie introduces 'football with a differance' to the guests

TOM: Football.
REGGIE: I think it's been done, Tom.
TOM: With a difference. No aggro, no fouls, no tension, no violence.
REGGIE: That's certainly not been done. Very good, Tom. What's the secret?
TOM: No opposition! We use skill, passing, teamwork and tactics. It's pure football.
REGGIE: Absolutely. This is exactly the sort of thing we've been looking for. And we've got the perfect opportunity to try it: the eleven of us against nobody.

hundreds of people flocking to the commune.

Another new member of staff is McBlane, the indecipherable Scottish chef, whose fierce appearance frightens everyone, even Reggie, although he avoids admitting it.

With a fortnight to go until opening day, Reggie wants to intensify the training and calls for new ideas. Tom suggests a unique form of football.

At the end of their trial game Tom – who is referee – is disappointed because they threw away their early advantage and winning only 4-1 was not enough.

The training continues well much to Reggie's delight. Soon it is opening day and the commune welcomes its first guest: Mr

Babbacombe, an undertaker. Little does he know that at the moment he is the only visitor. Mr Babbacombe has enrolled at the commune because he feels his profession has caused him to be an outcast. The guest is also eager to meet the other visitors, who are in short supply. To make him feel at home, some of the staff (Elizabeth, Doc, C.J., David and Joan) pretend to be guests, but things do not go to plan.

When Doc Morrisey is pretending to be a guest, things get confusing and he stands up when Reggie asks Jimmy, who is pretending to be the Doc, a question. Realising what he has done, he explains himself.

Doc: I think I should explain why I got up just now. Uh . . . I'm prey to a delusion that I'm a

James Warrior

Character: Mr Babbacombe, undertaker.
Series 3, Episode 2.
Born: Ammanford.
Training: Guild Hall School of Music and Drama.
Early Career: Dustman, builder.
Credits include: TV – Budgie, The Sweeney, London's Burning, All Creatures Great and Small, Heartbeat, Kavanagh QC.

Leslie Sands

Character: Thruxton Appleby, textiles tycoon.
Series 3, Episode 2.
Born: Bradford.
Education: English at Leeds University.
Credits include: TV – Z Cars, Cluff (title role).
Update: Successful writer. First part of autobiography published in 1990.
P.S. Also made a myriad of theatrical appearances, including time with RSC and National Theatre.

'I REMEMBER . . . I played a chap walking a dog on the canal towpath while Jimmy and Reggie were stuck on a barge. I only had two lines to say and got them wrong. We had to do a retake. Instead of: "All my best to Curly," I said: "Charlie. But it was a nice little scene and after we'd finished we had lunch on the barge.'
(Stewart Quentin Holmes)

'I enjoyed playing Mr Babbacombe. I've played a lot of Welshmen for David Nobbs over the years. When I was offered the part, I said I'd do anything David's written because it's bound to be funny.

'I'd watched the earlier series and was a fan like half the country. One thing that caught on very quickly was all the little catchphrases, something David's good at doing. You ended up recognising these characters because each of them had their own idiosyncracies.'
(James Warrior)

member of the medical profession. Uh . . . it's embarrassing, if anyone says is there a doctor in the house, I say: 'Yes, I'm a doctor, make way, make way.'

Then when I get to the scene of the disaster they say: 'Oh, thank God you've arrived, Doc.' Then I say: 'I just remembered, I'm not a doctor.'

The disasters continue. Elizabeth and Joan get confused when Reggie asks Mrs Naylor a question, and David Harris-Jones stands up in his black sunglasses, gaudy waistcoat and necklaces, and explains his problem is drugs.

Mr Babbacombe suddenly recognises David as the warden and realises everyone else seated on the guests' chairs are members of staff too. When he learns he is the only guest at present, he is too embarrassed to stay. The commune has got off to a poor start, but things will pick up

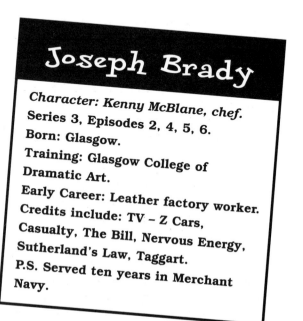

Joseph Brady

Character: Kenny McBlane, chef.
Series 3, Episodes 2, 4, 5, 6.
Born: Glasgow.
Training: Glasgow College of Dramatic Art.
Early Career: Leather factory worker.
Credits include: TV – Z Cars, Casualty, The Bill, Nervous Energy, Sutherland's Law, Taggart.
P.S. Served ten years in Merchant Navy.

John Horsley

DOC MORRISEY

Doc Morrisey was employed as company doctor at Sunshine Desserts. Not only was he totally useless but also a hypochondriac who always suffered more ailments than his patients. Reggie once described him as the 'wizard of the Aspirin' because of his incompetence and penchant for prescribing the tablet for any illness encountered.

The Doc was a nice enough guy: he was affable, harmless and caring, but he had never been one of life's success stories. It was a miracle he had actually graduated as a doctor, particularly when he confessed that many new parts of the body had been invented since he qualified.

His reputation was such that he was never too busy at Sunshine Desserts, but Doc was never happier than when Joan Greengross turned up to see him. He always fancied Joan and hoped she would occasionally feel chesty, allowing him the chance of examining her. Obsessed by the female form, Doc Morrisey often kept girlie mags in his drawer for those quieter moments of the day.

Doc's severe lack of confidence in his medical abilities was bruised even further when he was fired at C.J.'s fishing competition after diagnosing the host as dead when he had only fainted.

John Horsley often used to turn up on his motorbike.

By the beginning of series two the doctor had been reinstated at Sunshine Desserts because C.J. had entered a brief phase of realising the importance of loyalty and happiness. But life at the dessert giant had its wobbles and when Doc revealed Martin Wellbourne's true identity, C.J. sacked both Reggie and Doc. Fortunes took a further dive when he was struck off the medical register for gross professional incompetence for prescribing more of the 'white pills' for what turned out to be the first case of pink baboon fever to hit Chertsey.

Reggie never forgot his friends and employed Doc as Grot's Head of Forward Planning – although Reggie's ulterior motive was to recruit people in the wrong jobs to help destroy Grot. Being back in work was the stimulus Doc needed and rewarded his boss with a feast of ideas, including the amazingly successful January sales in September, with fantastic price increases.

After Grot the Doc adopted the title 'Professor' and taught English before Reggie offered another job, this time as the psychologist at the commune. When Perrins closed Doc went back to teaching calling himself Professor Morrisey again because that way he could attract higher hourly rates.

When veteran actor John Horsley read *The Legacy of Reginald Perrin* he noticed Doc Morrisey's life had changed very little in the twenty years since he first graced our screens.

'He was still eating Indian meals and living in a bedsit in Southall, above a shop selling Indian spices. Doc was always struggling to survive and I was pleased to see he was still the same ol' character.

'He's a great chap to play and, funnily enough, popular with real-life doctors, particularly with the constant worrying about his own health,' laughs John. 'I remember going to my doctor when the original series was on and as soon as I walked through the door, he smiled and said to me: "I can't help thinking of Doc Morrisey whenever I see you, and wonder why you're coming to me for advice."'

John found it easy bringing Doc Morrisey to life again, as did the rest of the cast, which is one reason filming the new series has gone so smoothly. 'From day one everything slotted into place, so much so that it was hard to believe we hadn't worked together as a group for nearly 20 years. In fact, things went so well that a couple of times Tim Preece and a few of us joked about starting an argument,' smiles John. 'That way we might frighten Gareth Gwenlan into thinking things weren't as rosy between us after all. But it wouldn't have worked because it was obvious to everyone, particularly Gareth, that everything was going well.'

John was born in 1920 at Westcliff-on-Sea, Essex. Ironically, his father was a doctor, while his mother a professional singer. In 1938 he left school and made his acting debut at the Theatre Royal, Bournemouth, earning 25 shillings a week.

'As far as I can remember, I've always wanted to act. I went to St Paul's School in London and although my successes at school were pretty sparse, the few I did have were connected to drama.'

After spending a year in various reps including Hastings, Eastbourne and Watford, John was conscripted into the army in 1940. During the war he served with the Devon Yeomanry in Italy and Sicily before contracting hepatitis. The remaining years were spent assigned to the ABCA Play Unit (Army Bureau Current Affairs Play Unit) touring England, France and Germany. 'It was quite a distinguished theatre company and gave me the opportunity to resume my acting. It was great experience and as I hadn't been to drama school I felt I learnt a lot about the trade by being involved.'

After the cessation of hostilities John was quickly employed back in the theatre. While at Salisbury Rep, he met his wife, actress June Marshall, whom he was married to for 40 years before her death.

Until the 1950s, John's career had been dominated by the stage, but the beginning of the new decade brought with it a fresh opportunity for the actor. 'I made my film debut in 1950's *Highly Dangerous*. Although I began making a lot more films from then on, I always tried maintaining a link with the theatre because I'd joined the profession to be a stage actor. However, appearing in the odd film was an ideal way of keeping one going between stints in the theatre.'

Other film roles included: *Appointment with Venus* with David Niven and Glynis

Johns; *The Long Memory* with John Mills; playing a detective with Frankie Howerd in *The Runaway Bus; Above Us the Waves* with John Mills again; *Hell Drivers* and *Ben Hur*.

John's big screen career has been dominated by the numerous war movies such as *Dunkirk* and *Sink the Bismarck!* that were piling out of the British film studios after the war. Whereas his film roles were predominantly serious, he played a lot of comedy on TV.

'I was in *Terry and June* and *You Rang, M'Lord?* in which I played Sir Ralph Shawcross for several series. But I've also been in *Z Cars; Softly, Softly; Dempsey and Makepeace; Robin of Sherwood; The Bill; Hot Metal*, where I played a priest; *Clayhanger* and *Kavanagh QC*, playing another judge.'

In a career spanning more than five decades, there is not much that John Horsley has not accomplished. In his early years he was often cast as policemen of varying rank and military men, but the advent of TV – which he worked in prodigiously from the 1950s – saw his range of character parts broaden to include all sorts of professionals: doctors, lawyers and judges – which he was doing in Crown Court when offered the part of Doc Morrisey. 'I was filming in Manchester when my agent called to let me know the BBC wanted to interview me about the role. I appeared in *Crown Court* quite a lot which meant I couldn't appear in every episode of Reggie Perrin – which was a shame.'

Now, in his mid-70s, John – who thinks he gets more like the Doc every day – is convinced the new series will attract a whole new audience to the Reggie Perrin legend. 'I'm sure people who never saw the original three series will enjoy what we've done; and the people who did see it will be able to identify with all the characters again, and, hopefully, become attached to them.'

EPISODE THREE:

"I didn't get where I am today without knowing that Perrins is the best thing since sliced bread." (C.J.)

"Case of the pot calling the kettle a silver lining." (C.J.)

Mr Babbacombe's departure has brought staff morale to an all-time low. In an attempt to raise the dejected bunch, Reggie reads out some of the adverts that will be hitting the market and generating a flood of guests.

A group session at the commune

"Perrins is super!"

"Perrins is a knockout!"

"Are you a backward reader? Then visit Snirrep."

"I didn't get where I am today without knowing that Perrins is the best thing since sliced bread."

"Lost all faith in experts? Then come to Perrins, guaranteed no experts in anything."

"Want to drop out, but don't like drop-outs? At Perrins the drop-outs are just like you: they're more like drop-ins; so next time you feel like dropping out, why not drop in?"

Joyce Windsor

Character: Mrs Hollies, complaining neighbour.
Series 3, Episode 2.
Born: London.
Training: RADA.
Credits include: TV – *Butterflies, Bread, Five Children and It.*
Update: Still working on the stage.

Thruxton Appleby, the textiles tycoon, who liked the Perrins adverts' 'bared-faced cheek'. Appleby sees the commune as his last chance to become more liked.

At the next staff meeting Reggie senses everyone is still feeling low. He wants his companions to cheer up because Perrins is on the verge of greatness.

Realising he has been taking too dominant a role, he promises to give everyone additional responsibility from now on.

More guests arrive and Mr Pelham and Thruxton Appleby are making fine progress. After an unsuccessful brief detour to try and tell McBlane the previous day's chicken curry was too hot, Reggie wanders round to see how the staff are getting on. First day nerves seem to be affecting everyone. Doc Morrisey is finding it difficult to get into his stride during a word association task with Bernard Trilling, head of comedy at a TV station, who has lost his sense of comedy. And David Harris-Jones infuriatingly stutters and stumbles his way through a

Reggie decides from now on to interview the applicants personally. To his surprise, Mr Pelham, the pig farmer, walks into his office. Although he has become very successful, highlighted by the fact that the local abattoir at Bicester gives him group rates, he has a big problem: he has gone off meat. Reggie, lacking his usual aplomb, promises to cure Mr Pelham at the commune.

The next guest Reggie interviews is

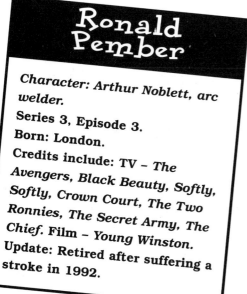

Ronald Pember

Character: Arthur Noblett, arc welder.
Series 3, Episode 3.
Born: London.
Credits include: TV – *The Avengers, Black Beauty, Softly, Softly, Crown Court, The Two Ronnies, The Secret Army, The Chief.* Film – *Young Winston.*
Update: Retired after suffering a stroke in 1992.

Sally Lahee

Character: Hilary Meadows, housewife, guest at commune.
Series 3, Episode 3.
Born: London.
Credits include: TV – *Dr Finlay's Casebook, The Newcomers, Crossroads, Duchess of Duke Street, May to December.*
Update: Now runs her own antiques business.

sex therapy session with the composed Hilary Meadows, only to find she has no sexual problems at all.

Meanwhile in Reggie's office, C.J. is conducting a role-play session in industrial negotiations with the belligerent Thruxton Appleby and Arthur Noblet, who is requesting additional fringe benefits at the Hardcastle Handbag Company. C.J. and Reggie begin by adopting observing roles as Cynthia Jones, Mr Appleby's secretary, and a man from the Industrial Relations Research Council, respectively.

Unhappy with the guests' performance, C.J. and Reggie step in to show how it should be done, or so they say, because they end up in a bitter argument – not the example to set.

By the end of the episode, Mr Appleby

Reggie made C.J. responsible for 'work' at the commune – a post well-suited to his famous managerial skills

and Mr Pelham are heading home, both satisfied with their progress, much to Reggie's surprise. Thruxton believes he is a new man and that he is well on the road to being likeable. To show his appreciation he pays Reggie £1000, whereas Mr Pelham, who is equally pleased with his stay at Perrins, donates a year's supply of pork chops.

By now the commune is thriving and next week's bookings show 12 new guests due to arrive.

'I REMEMBER . . . playing Thruxton Appleby was one of the most pleasant parts I played when I was younger and more active in the world of TV. Cheltenham – in the summer of '78 – took on a new and subtler meaning for me after working there with Leonard Rossiter.

'In the very popular show Leonard was surrounded by a group of talented and most likeable people who, under his leadership and assisted by a marvellous script, made my whole guest appearance a delight.'

(Leslie Sands)

Frederick Jaeger

Character: Bernard Trilling, head of comedy, Anaemia Television.
Series 3 Episode 3.
Born: Berlin.
Training: Guild Hall School of Music and Drama.
Credits include: TV – Some Mothers Do 'Ave 'Em, Special Branch, Yes, Minister.
Update: Hasn't stopped working for 40 years.
P.S. Worked with Leonard Rossiter and John Barron in rep at Preston and Hull in the 50s.

Reggie and C.J.

EPISODE FOUR:

"Sacrifice never killed a cat." (C.J.)

"I didn't get where I am today by realising you'd have a cock-up on the staffing front if you aren't a loyalty person." (Reggie)

Michael Segal

Character: Mr Jenkins, council planning officer.
Series 3, Episode 4.
Born: London.
Early career: Cabinetmaker.
Credits include: TV – *Inside Story, The Persuaders, The Return of the Saint, Minder.* Film – *Pay Roll, The Dirty Dozen, The Prisoner of Zenda.*
Update: Retired due to ill health.
P.S. His TV career began in children's programmes.

It is Christmas time and with 35 people in the community, Elizabeth feels festive jollities will be a thing of the past. She also wants to cook Christmas dinner and reckons Reggie will be scared to tell McBlane. Reggie adopts his tough image and assures Elizabeth that she should not worry about such petty things – he will sort it out. Little does she know that Reggie, like everyone else, is terrified of the aggressive, grubby Scotsman.

Next morning, he approaches McBlane

Reggie attempts to assert himself over McBlane

and after much fawning tries to broach the issue regarding cooking Christmas dinner. McBlane's wild gesturing with an assortment of vicious knives unnerves Reggie who, cowering away into the corner, manages to creep out of the kitchen with the matter unresolved.

Christmas passes uneventfully but successfully. The next problem to affect Elizabeth is the nightmarish sleeping arrangements – a sign of the commune's continuing success. Reggie decides there is only one option: staff must share rooms. For starters, he suggests C.J. and Doc Morrisey sharing. Elizabeth, convinced he will not be able to gain their agreement, lays a £5 bet on Reggie failing.

Reggie tackles C.J. first.

REGGIE: Well, C.J. Success is growing by the week.
C.J.: I knew it would, Reggie. It's a long lane that gathers no moss.
REGGIE: It certainly is, C.J. But success brings its own problems; people are going to have to make sacrifices.
C.J.: Glad to hear it. Sacrifice never killed a cat.
REGGIE: It certainly didn't, C.J. I want you to share your bedroom with McBlane.

C.J.: Yes . . . what! Ah . . . Reg . . .
(C.J. is physically shocked and starts clutching at Reggie's desk and his coloured telephones.)
REGGIE: I think I know what you're trying to say, C.J. Careful, careful, you're on red. I think what you're trying to say is you didn't get where you are today by sleeping with sweaty Caledonian chefs. I didn't realise you'd feel quite so strongly about it, C.J., so I'll tell you what I'll do: you can share with Doc Morrisey instead.
C.J.: Oh, thank you, Reggie, thank you. I appreciate that . . . oh, thank you, thank you, Reggie.

When C.J. learns he can share with the Doc instead, relief sweeps over his face and he accepts the idea admirably. Things do not go quite as well with Doc Morrisey who faints at the thought of sharing with his former boss, meaning Elizabeth wins the bet.

At the next staff meeting, Reggie announces that with 38 guests now attending the commune, space is at a premium and the sheds in which activities are carried out will be converted into bedrooms, with all activities transferring to the appropriate bedrooms.

Reggie detects a threat on the horizon when Mr Dent from the local council's planning office asks to visit. Afraid that he will be searching for a reason to close the commune down, Reggie tries all the tricks to distract the official, including offering

Janet Davies

Character: Ethel Merman, housewife.
Series 3, Episode 4.
Born: Wakefield.
Credits include: TV – Dad's Army (Mavis Pike), Last of the Summer Wine, The Professionals, General Hospital. Film – Under Milk Wood. Theatre – The Love Match.
Update: Died in 1987.

David Ellison

Character: Factory owner, guest at commune.
Series 3, Episode 4.

him an excessive number of ginger nut biscuits with his coffee.

By the end of the meeting, Reggie has turned Mr Dent from being an overambitious creep eager to spot the slightest discrepancy in the running of

Peter Schofield

Character: Mr Winstanley, Mr Dent's boss.
Series 3, Episode 4.
Born: Leyland.
Training: Bradford Northern Theatre School.
Credits include: TV – Suntrap (by David Nobbs), Airline, Some Mother's Do 'Ave 'Em.
Update: Recently finished 2-year tour of Me and My Girl.

Robert Gillespie

Character: Mr Dent, planning officer.
Series 3, Episode 4.
Born: Lille, France.
Training: RADA.
Credits include: TV – Jesus of Nazareth, Rising Damp, Keep it in the Family (5 series), Whatever Happened to the Likely Lads, George and Mildred, Dad's Army.

Perrins, into a willing guest at the commune.

The following day Mr Dent attends his first group session. Amongst the other guests is a factory owner who admits to being a 'raving poof'; an insurance salesman who has lost his motivation to sell; a housewife from Gravesend who everybody believes is the internationally famous Ethel Merman; a conman called Edwards, who is currently selling a bag of invisible trout; and a shy vet.

Later that day, Tom tells Reggie about a problem he is experiencing with his new form of football.

TOM: My football with each team playing for the opponents against themselves isn't working perfectly, Reggie. It's failed to remove the aggression. Since each team plays entirely for the opponents they become the opponents who become them; and they kick the living daylights out of each other just as they always did.
REGGIE: Well you must keep on trying, Tom. What you must do is persist, see, Tom. Persistence, persistence, persistence (punching his fist into the palm of other hand). That's it.

TOM: Reggie, eureka. When you bashed your fists like that you gave me an idea. I've solved the problem. I've taken the aggression out of sport.
REGGIE: There you are, Tom, I told you you'd come up with something. What is it?
TOM: Boxing.
REGGIE: Boxing? I think events have moved too fast for you again, Tom. Boxing has been invented.
TOM: With a difference: non-aggressive boxing.
REGGIE: That certainly hasn't been invented.

Reggie receives a visit from Mr Winstanley, an official from Botchley Borough Council's Planning Office, who is searching for the elusive Mr Dent who vanished after visiting the commune. Reggie tells Dent's superior that he is a guest at the commune and is taking part in a boxing match that very afternoon. Mr Winstanley finds this hard to believe. He finds the match even more difficult to believe because Mr Dent and the other fighter are

Bunny May

Character: Insurance salesman, who has lost his motivation to sell, commune guest.
Series 3, Episode 4.

fighting themselves. A very funny scene.

After watching Mr Wilkins beat himself by a knockout and Mr Dent win against himself on points, it is not long before Mr Winstanley is also residing at the commune. Two more council employees visit, and two more council officials sign up on the guests' list.

The evening passes with a communal singing event. Spirits are high, tensions are non-existent and Perrins is progressing well. In bed Reggie tells Elizabeth that he is deeply content and happy (probably for the first time during his working life) but still a little worried about whether this happiness can last.

'I REMEMBER . . . I enjoyed working with Leonard, although he did have an abrasive quaity. Jonathan Lynn, who directed him in *Loot* – the play in which he died – once said to me: "You always knew if Leonard Rossiter was a friend of yours by the amiable way that he would insult you."'
(John Horsley)

ABOVE RIGHT: Reggie with Mr Dent
BELOW RIGHT: Reggie with Mr Winstanley, Mr. Dent's boss

Andrew Johns

Character: Mr Pennell, local council employee.
Series 3, Episode 4.
Born: London.
Training: RADA.
Credits include: TV – *Julius Caesar, Doctor Who.*
Update: Recent work includes numerous corporate training videos and commercials.

Peter Hill

Character: Conman.
Series 3, Episode 4.
Credits: TV – *Crossroads* (Arthur Browlow).
Update: Died in 1995.

Sally-Jane Spencer

LINDA PATTERSON

Linda – Reggie's curvaceous blonde daughter – was the wife of gangly Tom, and mother of the terrible duo: Adam and Jocasta. Other than a brief spell at the commune, where she became the art therapist, Linda – with her plunging necklines – had not pursued a particular career after leaving school. In fact, she never had the chance, because she had her work cut out raising her two children and looking after her pompous husband.

Linda's happy-go-lucky and, at times, slightly dotty personality was often at odds with Tom's somewhat prickly manner, and it's surprising their marriage survived as long as it did

The only thing Tom and Linda seemed to have in common was that they both possessed open pores which meant they sweated profusely. Other than that, Linda often got frustrated with her hubby's priggish attitudes and excessive use of embarrassing terms of endearment, including: 'Squelchypoos', 'Squashyboobs', 'Lindipops' and 'Lindisquirts'.

By the beginning of series four, Linda and Tom are divorced and have not spoken to each other for seven years. But realising life's not the same without each other to love, they remarry.

Because Sally-Jane Spencer found the scripts of Reggie Perrin funny and extremely unusual compared with anything else around at the time, she had no doubts about accepting the part of Linda, and remembers her interview with producer Gareth Gwenlan well.

'I sat in Gareth's office and read one little scene where Uncle Jimmy and Linda arrive at Reggie's home. I remember everything so clearly – even the clothes I wore.

'The three years spent working on the original three series turned out to be the happiest of my career: we had lots of fun; lots of laughs; and everyone was delightful to work with.'

When Sally-Jane regrouped with the rest of the cast for the new series, she could not get over the feeling she experienced. 'It was just like *This Is Your Life.* Everyone was so thrilled to be back together. We first met for the read-through and as everybody arrived they were greeted with the sort of reaction one sees every week on Michael Aspel's show - it was amazing.

'For me, it feels just like coming home,' she explains. 'Everything was familiar: the BBC studio, the cast and some faces involved in the production. Doing the new Reggie Perrin is the icing on the cake as far as my career's concerned.'

Sally-Jane was born in Buckinghamshire. Her father is a film producer so it came as no great shock when she showed early signs of wanting to follow his example and make a career out of the acting profession.

She studied at Elmhurst, the drama

school whose other graduates have included Hayley Mills, Jenny Agutter, Fiona Fullerton and Tessa Wyatt.

After Elmhurst, Sally-Jane began her thespian life in style: instead of the usual apprenticeship in endless repertory companies around the country, she went straight into the West End production of *The Prime of Miss Jean Brodie*, where she stayed a year. Like many actresses launching their careers, she spent her early years working in the theatre. 'I did various bits and pieces including four seasons at Chichester doing all sorts of prestigious plays. But whereas my theatrical career was dominated by drama, my TV career has consisted largely of comedy,' says Sally-Jane.

However, there were exceptions, and for just over two years in the late 60s, she played Margot Kerr in the BBC drama *The Newcomers*, along with a cast including Alan Browning, Gladys Henson and Judy Geeson. The twice-weekly soap focused on a London family's struggle to settle into their new lives in Angleton, a fictitious Suffolk village.

But Sally-Jane's acting career has been dominated by the success of Reggie Perrin. 'Until then I'd worked on some nice productions but nothing matched the success of playing Linda.' Naturally, she jumped at the opportunity of playing the character again.

'Before Gareth called, I kept getting people coming up to me and asking: "I've read there's going to be a new series of Reggie, when does it start?" I had to tell them I didn't have a clue.'

Shortly after, the call arrived from Gareth Gwenlan and Sally-Jane agreed to step into Linda's shoes once again. 'Because of the wonderful cast and David Nobbs's brilliant scripts, I knew instinctively that agreeing to do another series was the right move.'

The fourth series of Reggie did not mean Sally-Jane would be resuming just the life of a particular character, it also resulted in the bubbly actress picking up her acting career after a break of over a decade.

Shortly after finishing the third series, Sally-Jane got married and raised two children which meant that – except for the occasional small part – she has been away from the business – but she's pleased to be back.

'It's great to be acting again, and now my children are a reasonable age – Emily's 15 and Timothy's 13 – I can concentrate on picking up my career from where I left off before my break.'

Linda and Tom Patterson in Series Four

EPISODE FIVE:

"Food is dullsville Arizona!" (Tony)

"Out of the mouths of babes and little children."   (C.J.)

Frank Baker

Character: *The shy vet.*
Series 3, Episodes 4, 5.
Born: *London.*
Credits include: *TV – Reilly –Ace of Spies, Hannay, The Chief, Paparazzo, Pie in the Sky.*
Film – *The Secret Garden, Yentl.*

New faces continue flocking to Perrins. Latest guests include: a 'sub-human moron' called Glen Higgins; Elton Johnson, a black school teacher; sexy Deborah Swaffham and Clive 'Lofty' Anstruther, Jimmy's ex-mate who claims he is a sucker and always being taken for a ride. Reggie quickly remembers he ripped Jimmy off while they were trying to set up a private army. He is also a fraud because he was never a colonel in the army like he told Jimmy.

Donning tracksuits, Reggie gees up his team and seeks new ideas to keep the whole philosophy of Perrins fresh. Jimmy suggests Perrins Peacekeeping Force; Tom's idea is solo tennis while C.J. motions an idea for ending words with 'urgle', which is put to the test on the Tube.

REGGIE: Eleven minutes lateurgle.
C.J.: Typicalurgle.
JOHNSON: Not a bad morningurgle.
DEBORAH: A bit coldurgle.
HIGGINS: Enough to freeze the burgles off a brass monkurgle.
LOFTY: Looks like rainurgle.

Peter Roberts

Character: Youth, guest at commune.
Series 3, Episode 5.

Vincent Brimble

Character: Glenn Higgins, yob.
Series 3, Episode 5.

The commune is not providing Reggie with the contentment and peace he yearns for in life

Back at the commune, P.C. Potts notices he has been robbed of £15, at which point the quietly spoken shy vet claims he lost £10 yesterday. When the number of thefts reaches five, Reggie agrees to do nothing so long as the culprit returns everything. The stealing continues and when Reggie suggests everyone leaves their valuables out the following night, the result is £382, four watches, three rings and two bracelets are pinched. It seems nothing is sacred from the decay and miseries associated with modern society. Reggie's concerns about whether his contentment would last seem to be coming true.

Because of the thefts, several guests decide it is time to leave, including Clive

Kenneth Watson

Character: Superintendent Potts, guest at commune.
Series 3, Episode 5.
Training: RADA.
Credits include: TV – *The Brothers, Take the High Road, Emmerdale Farm, Coronation Street* **(Ralph Lancaster),** *Wycliffe, Dixon of Dock Green, Crown Court.*

DEBORAH: Or even snowurgle.
C.J.: I didn't gurgle where I am todurgle without recognising a murgle that looks like snow when I see one.
(All the passengers give up their seats and move away.)
REGGIE: That's one way of getting all the seats.
OTHERS: Absoluteurgle.
REGGIE: That's all right, you can stop now – they've all gone.

Terence Alexander

Character: Clive 'Lofty' Anstruther, Jimmy's partner.
Series 3, Episode 5.
Born: London.
Credits include: TV – *The Pallisers, Terry and June, The Avengers, Bergerac* **(Charlie Hungerford). Film –** *The Green Man, Carry On Regardless, The League of Gentlemen.*
Update: Semi-retired but records coffee commercials for Norwegian TV. P.S. Considered being a priest, journalist and surgeon before deciding to become an actor aged sixteen.

Leslie Glazer

Character: Merchant banker, guest at commune.
Series 3, Episode 5.
Born: London.
Credits include: Theatre – a stint at the Old Vic.
Update: Was also a successful playwright. Died in 1995.

'Lofty' Anstruther. But not before he has made time to write a letter admitting he carried out the thefts. Reggie's rage is calmed by Elizabeth in her normal unruffled manner when she tells him not to dwell on yesterday's problems and to move on.

During the next staff meeting Reggie detects that, once again, morale is at a low ebb. The nub of the problem is Deborah Swaffham, who, unbeknown to their wives, has been flirting with the male staff and inviting them to her bedroom. When further disagreements erupt it is Elizabeth who brings the meeting to order, concluding that

Gordon Case

Character: Johnson, teacher, guest at commune.
Series 3, Episode 5.
Born: Guyana.
Credits include: TV – *Play for Today, Spearhead*.
Update: Most of his work is in the theatre.

Hilary Tindall

Character: Deborah Swaffham, guest at commune.
Series 3, Episode 5.
Born: Manchester.
Training: RADA.
Early career: Dressmaker.
Credits include: TV – *The Brothers, Tales of the Unexpected, Max Headroom*.
Theatre – *The Glass Menagerie, A Street Car Named Desire*.
Update: Died in 1992.

the only answer is to send Ms Swaffham to David, the sex therapist, who is aghast at the suggestion. Elizabeth also encourages the staff to brush aside menial issues and refocus on the commune's objectives.

Further problems shake the infrastructure of Perrins when David succumbs to the flirtatious advances of Deborah, and heads off to her bedroom only to be spotted by loving wife, Prue. The result is Prue leaving David and the commune and heading home to her mother's in order to reassess her marital life.

The strife continues. More guests leave. Can the commune survive?

'I REMEMBER . . . . I just floated in and out because my role as one of the guests was small. But as an old-seasoned pro I could see everyone was ticking away like a Swish watch.

'For someone like me who wanders through the periphery of TV, appearing in the Reggie Perrin series was like coming home.'
(Kenneth Watson)

'When I saw the script I knew straight away that Clive 'Lofty' Anstruther was a smashing part. Leonard Rossiter contributed an enormous amount to the show's success, but even the roles normally classed as small parts came over as very important. There wasn't a weak link in it which is important in sitcoms.

'My guest role was a strongly written character who was woven into the fabric of the story although he only appeared once.

'In those days, directors would often phone and say: "It isn't a wonderful part but I know you can make something of it." My heart always sank when I heard those words because it meant it was a nothing part and you had to try to rescue it. With 'Lofty' all I had to do was find a way of saying the lines and simply do it – it was as easy as that.'
(Terence Alexander)

Joan Peart

Character: Mrs E. Blythe-Erpingham, haughty neighbour.
Series 3, Episode 5.
Born: London.
Credits include: TV – *General Hospital*.
Update: After a career dominated by the stage, she died in 1989.
PS. She was married to John Barron who played C.J.

EPISODE SIX:

"I didn't get where I am today by looking a gift horse in the mouth or by going down with a sinking ship." (C.J.)

"I'm not hitting any more revolting drinks unless it leads to results city Arizona." (Tony)

Reggie's problems continue. Mrs E Blythe-Erpingham brings a petition signed by 1276 residents complaining about a myriad of things to Reggie's home. Fed up with the neighbouring moaners, he rips the petition up.

Later in a pub Reggie meets a depressing, miserable landlord and insults him. Then he returns home to find 22 more guests have left the commune. Elizabeth, recognising the symptoms, is worried that Reggie's actions are leading to self-destruction just like his time at Sunshine Desserts and Grot. He denies his finger is heading for the self-destruct button.

When Reggie returns to his office later in the day, he finds Doc Morrisey staring at a water sample by the window. The Doc feels his new invention is the answer to all of Reggie's problems, but his less than impressive medical record does not install much confidence in Reggie.

REGGIE: Oh, Doc, sorry. Didn't know you were there else I wouldn't have sighed. The fact that 40 more guests have left: nothing to sigh about is there? Nothing to be gloomy about is there? That isn't a crisis is it?
DOC: Never mind, Reggie; every hour of need throws up a hero.
REGGIE: But who, Doc, who?
DOC: Me.

REGGIE: You?
DOC: Yes! (He passes the water to Reggie.)
REGGIE: This?
DOC: Yes, taste it, Reggie.
REGGIE: It doesn't taste of anything, Doc.
DOC: That tasteless, colourless liquid achieves by chemical means all the good you are trying to bring to people in your community. Confidence is waning, Reggie. With one stroke that wonder potion can revive it.
REGGIE: British invention is it, Doc?
DOC: I invented it.
REGGIE: Oh. (He puts the water down.)
DOC: I can detect a lack of confidence in you now, Reggie, and it pains me. Where's your faith and trust?

Later, Doc Morrisey introduces his new potion, which has only been tested so far on HB pencils, to the rest of the team. He claims it will 'control our adrenalin, insulin, blood supply, sugar levels, cures all aggression and inhibitions and regular doses keep our bodies in a state of equilibrium.' When he asks for volunteers to try it there is a deathly silence. Eventually, after much badgering by their leader, all the staff sample Doc's magic liquid.

By dinner time all 23 guests and the entire staff, bar Reggie, the Doc, Tony and Jimmy have fallen ill thanks to dysentery. During the meal the lone quartet is gradually whittled down until the dining room is empty. Although Doc gets the blame because of his potion, he tells Reggie it is impossible: his experiment was psychological not medically based because the drink was only water.

Reggie is down in the dumps because it seems one problem after another is hitting the commune. Unable to stand the thought of another communal evening, he pops out to a nearby pub where he bumps into

Seamus Finnegan, who supplies even more grim news.

Thugs who fell victim to Jimmy's militaristic peace-keeping force are scheming to attack Perrins on Saturday. Reggie tells the staff at the following day's staff meeting. He suggests defending the commune from the louts and appoints Jimmy as leader for the task.

Next morning, Prue returns to help and Jimmy – dressed in full military uniform – airs his proposed plans. After dismissing ideas for disguising themselves as molehills and compost heaps, he opts for trees.

It feels like a long night dressed up as trees in the front garden waiting for the trouble to begin. At midnight, thinking the yobs are not coming, everyone goes inside to celebrate. Within minutes the battle begins with the smashing of windows.

The following day, the *Daily Grunge* headlines read: 'Revenge Gang Shatter Perrin Community.' Passing all the 'For Sale' signs outside all the Perrins' houses, is an ambulance dropping off the casualties. Most of the staff, including Tom, have broken limbs. The end of the commune is near.

'I REMEMBER . . . a horrendous night shoot with everyone dressed up as trees. I still shudder when I think about it. We had lots of trouble with the neighbours because it went on until about four in the morning when we should have finished at midnight.'
(Gareth Gwenlan)

Doc Morrisey shows Reggie his new invention

Reggie picks up green and red

'I only said a few lines but my heart sank when I saw the script because it read: "Reggie enters the pub which is broken down and decrepit, as is the landlord." During rehearsals I said my lines and Leonard followed up with a couple. When we had finished, he looked at me with a smile, and said: "You must be exhausted, you'd better have a sit down!"'

(Jonathan Fryer)

Jonathan Fryer

Character: Landlord, George and Dragon.
Series 3, Episode 6.
Born: London.
Training: Bournemouth Drama School.
Credits include: TV – *Z Cars*, *Keeping Up Appearances*, *Target*.
Update: Now a busy after-dinner speaker.

Leslie Adams

Character: Driver, spots guests dressed as trees.
Series 3, Episode 6.
Born: Bramhall.
Early career: Dentist.
Credits include: TV – Friends to Tea, Varietea (both his own shows).
Update: Died in 1993.
P.S. Spent most of his career touring variety theatres.

Leslie Schofield

TOM PATTERSON
SERIES THREE

Tom arrived at the commune after failing to secure another job in advertising. Since his last appointment as Grot's Head of Publicity, he had caught the old English crafts bug and hoped to be given the role of craft's therapist at Perrins. But Reggie had him earmarked as the sport's therapist – something Tom thought he was unsuitable for – and wanted him to eliminate competition and aggression from sport. His successes before the commune's demise included ridding aggression from football by playing with no opposition, and from boxing by getting opponents to box themselves.

When Leslie was offered the part of Tom in the third series - replacing the unavailable Tim Preece - he was delighted but also scared stiff.

'My agent asked me to go and see Gareth Gwenlan. Obviously he didn't want to change the Tom character too much and was searching for a vague lookalike. During the interview I had no idea that was his intention until he began asking whether I could say things in a certain way; I then knew what he was after.'

Within an hour Leslie had been offered the part, but it was only then that he began appreciating the amount of responsibility he was taking on. 'I was very worried. Taking over a character who's already been created is much more difficult than creating something from new, even if you have plenty of material to work with.'

Stepping into Tim Preece's shoes was an unenviable and almost impossible task, especially when Leslie's predecessor had made a tremendous success of the part - thanks partly to his looks. Tim's portrayal of Tom anchored firmly on a degree of pomposity helped along by his appearance. Leslie's appearance, meanwhile, seemed too homely and considerate to carry the weight of Tom's awkward and stubborn personality.

TV history has proven that replacing key members of the cast at the beginning of a series rarely works, and – with no disrespect to the efforts of the talented Leslie Schofield – this situation was no exception. Although Leslie's performance was admirable, Tim Preece's familiar face was deeply missed. Leslie explains the difficulties he faced.

'I felt very restricted playing Tom simply because I inherited the character, leaving little scope to inject anything new. The cast members made me welcome from the start, especially Sue Nicholls whom I'd worked

Leslie Schofield (left) as Tom Patterson in Series Three. Tom, Reggie and Tony Webster return from playing Tom's 'football with a difference'

with previously on *Rentaghost*. The characters they played were real oddballs, which, of course, was the heart and soul of the series.

'Reggie was a very funny series and stupendously written. There's nothing around to touch it and as far as I'm concerned, British comedy is in full retreat. Nowadays we rely too much on camping everything up which suggests the script isn't funny enough or the characters aren't strong enough. Although many of the characters in Reggie Perrin were odd, you could at least say: "I've met nutters like that!"

'There was a great reality about the series, and Reggie's wife, Elizabeth, is a good example: you don't find anyone more conventional than the character Pauline Yates played; she was the only sane one amid the mayhem happening around her.'

One of Leslie's more vivid memories of his time on the show was playing cricket. But this time, instead of it being on location, like Tim Preece remembers, it was in the corridor at the BBC. I played with Trevor Adams and Bruce Bould, and it was quite a violent game with a tennis ball being whacked about the corridor. Things got so competitive we were banned from the corridor by the security.

'After elbowing cricket we invented a sort of curling on the wonderfully polished floors. We took turns in rolling a marble along the floor with the aim of getting it to stop on a particular tile. It became such an obsession we started doing it in the rehearsal room as well!'

Leslie, born in Oldham, showed an inkling of what the future had in store during school. He was often invited to the front of the class to tell stories he invented as he went along. 'I always wanted people to like me and applaud which is where it all began, I suppose.'

His early years were spent with grandparents and Leslie reflects on what turned out to be a lonely childhood. 'My parents divorced when I was young which was a very traumatic time. In those days it was difficult to divorce and one had to make one's own grounds before it could happen. I remember my father travelling to Brighton to employ a private detective to help him get the divorce through – it was the sort of thing you read about in books.'

The split affected Leslie at school and he entered a rebellious phase which included stealing. 'I was going off the rails and my father thought I was heading for approved school, so quickly decided I needed to learn some discipline.

'I spent two years on a naval training ship which was hard work but enjoyable. It also gave me an insight into what life in the Royal Navy would be like and I ended up doing ten years in the Fleet Air Arm.'

While serving in the navy Leslie got involved in acting in plays, two of which won drama festivals. One of the adjudicators was attached to the British Drama League and during a conversation Leslie told him he had decided he wanted to become an actor. 'I remember to this day the words he said. He replied: "I'm not saying you're going to be star, but I think you could make a good living out of it." That prompted me to raise the £96 – which was a fortune in those days – to buy myself out of the navy.'

Shortly after joining civvy street at the age of 26, Leslie was offered a small part in a play heading for the Edinburgh Festival. From there Leslie was recruited by an agent and spent a year in Eastbourne before heading off all over the country with various theatrical companies.

His TV career began thanks to an audition on the telephone in the late 60s. 'It was for the BBC series *The Troubleshooters*,' says Leslie. 'I was rehearsing for a live TV play for Thames when my agent phoned to tell me this BBC producer was interested in me playing a Texan troubleshooter in the series.'

Because his agent had told the producer Leslie had a marvellous American accent, he wanted to speak to him on the telephone. 'I had to phone the BBC and speak Texan from the moment someone picked up the telephone - I've never felt such a prat in all my life!' laughs Leslie. But it was worth it because within half an hour, the job was his.

Other TV credits include seven episodes in Granada's *Spoils of War*, playing a man who returned from the war a wreck after spending years in a Japanese War Camp; the children's programme *Johnny Briggs;* Jill Gascoine's husband in an episode of *The Gentle Touch* and a brief stint in *Coronation Street*. Leslie is still regularly seen on the small screen and on stage.

EPISODE SEVEN:

**"Be thorough, leave no worm unturned."
(C.J.)**

"Chow City, Arizona."   (Tony)

The final episode, or so everybody thought, had strands of sadness running throughout. The commune had ceased trading; all the properties associated with Perrins were up for sale; staff members – all of whom had become close and loyal friends of Reggie and Elizabeth – were leaving; and for Reggie, the creator of this close-knit community, a dream was over.

In many ways, the commune was the only time in Reggie's rollercoaster life that he had given himself wholeheartedly to a venture. In Sunshine Desserts he found himself caught up in the monotony and routine of life, which eventually became unbearable, while the Grot era was almost a vehicle for taking a swipe at Society's materialistic attitudes. But the formation of Perrins was a positive move for Reggie because he genuinely wanted to do something constructive and valuable for mankind. Sadly, it was not strong enough to survive the wave of difficulties life threw at it.

As Reggie clears his office the sad farewells begin. Doc Morrisey, who will return to his English tutoring while retaining the unearned status of professor

The last days of the commune

because it commands higher fees, almost breaks down with the overwhelming sadness of the occasion.

Tony and Joan – clad in motorbike leathers – are next to say their goodbyes, followed by the inimitable C.J. Jimmy, meanwhile, is heading for the Alps and probably another failure because he is relying on yet another of those so-called 'top drawer' friends of his who are nothing but unpredictable and untrustworthy. Nigel 'Ginger' Carstairs runs a chair lift in Switzerland and wants Jimmy to become a partner.

David and Prue – with baby Reggie – acknowledge their wandering days are over and are joining the family firm at Haverford West, while Tom will resume his life as an estate agent.

The departure of Reggie's little troupe of followers marks another shift in his life: it has shown that life goes on and everyone who always appeared so dependent on Reggie for almost everything, including guidance and work, no longer need him. The inevitable collapse of Perrins has meant reassessment of lives and they have all been able to make firm decisions about their futures. The same must now happen for Reggie.

After a spell on the dole Reggie is recruited by Amalgamated Aerosols. On his first day, no sooner has he left his house than everything reminds him of an existence from which he tried so desperately to escape. Life appears to have turned full circle because here he is plodding along the streets dressed in his office attire on his way to the commuters' train for London. The only differences are the road names: Leibnitz Drive, Bertrand Russell Rise and Schopenhauer Grove.

The managing director of the aerosol firm is F.J., C.J.'s brother who uses all the old tricks including the farting visitors' chairs.

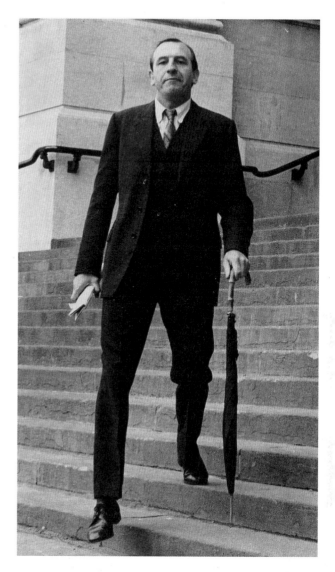

Reggie returns to office life, this time at Amalgamated Aerosols

Worst news is to come when Reggie finds out his immediate boss is, once again, C.J. Life certainly is a vicious circle!

Recruited as C.J.'s 'think tank', he is given two fervent assistants: Muscroft and Rosewall, yet another pair of commerce's yes-men. All the niggling aspects of life's bureaucratic routines are back in place – and Reggie knows it only too well.

While sharing a train ride with just

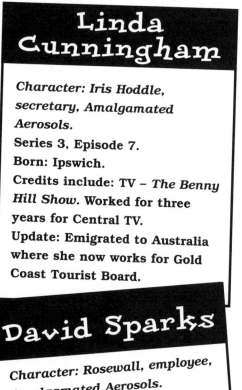

Linda Cunningham

Character: Iris Hoddle, secretary, Amalgamated Aerosols.
Series 3, Episode 7.
Born: Ipswich.
Credits include: TV – *The Benny Hill Show*. Worked for three years for Central TV.
Update: Emigrated to Australia where she now works for Gold Coast Tourist Board.

David Sparks

Character: Rosewall, employee, Amalgamated Aerosols.
Series 3, Episode 7.
Born: West Bromwich.
Training: Birmingham Theatre School, LAMDA.
Early career: British Rail.
Credits include: TV – *Redcap, Crossroads, Dangerfield, 999.*
Update: Returned to acting in 1993 after nine years as manager at publishing/advertising company.

another group of lifeless commuters, he stands up and preaches:

'Do you Reginald Iolanthe Perrin take British Rail's Southern Region for all your dreaded life? For better, for worse, for fuller, for dirtier, in lateness and in cancellation to retirement or phased redundancy do you part? "I do, I have to." Place this ring of dirt around your neck, it will be there everyday.'

When C.J. wants Reggie to familiarise himself with aerosols he sends him on a smelling at Borehamwood. When it comes to judging what each aerosol smells like, Reggie cannot resist the temptation to have some fun – it saves getting bored.

Next day Reggie and Elizabeth follow the same pattern but with a slight but significant difference. Elizabeth tells Reggie she hopes he has a nice day at the office, he replies 'I won't!' as normal, kisses his wife as normal, but then returns for a second more meaningful kiss. His goodbye also sounds a touch more serious this time, which Elizabeth senses.

En route to work Reggie constantly questions himself about why he did it and continuously apologises. After C.J. gives him the rather unusual results of yesterday's smelling, in which one person stated all the smells reminded him/her of a Bolivian unicyclist's jockstrap, Reggie is asked to investigate the matter. But there is no need because he dictates a memo to his new secretary, the blonde Miss Hoddle.

To all those present at the colander smelling:
Someone at the smelling wrote down that every air freshener smelt of a Bolivian unicyclist's jockstrap. After considerable research I have discovered who this idiot was: it was me, I did it. Not only did I do it, but I am glad I did it.

I will now tell you why I did it – and I choose my words very carefully. I did it because I find the whole thing fish slice. I will go further than that: I find it utterly and totally egg whisk.

Reginald I. Perrin.

Reggie begins daydreaming about the time he faked his suicide. He keeps picturing himself running across that Dorset beach stripping off (the opening credits). He picks up the phone and asks his secretary to check on train times to the Dorset coast. The inevitable has happened again: Reggie folds his arms, leans back in his chair, closes his eyes and prepares for another trip south.

John Quayle

Character: Mr Fennel, personnel manager, Amalgamated Aerosols.
Series 3, Episode 7.
Born: Lincoln.
Training: RADA.
Credits include: TV – *Terry and June, Upstairs, Downstairs, Duchess of Duke Street, Nanny.* **Theatre –** *Watch on the Rhine.*

'I REMEMBER . . . my character, McBlane, very well because he talked in gobbledygook. Although my last appearance was in the penultimate episode, I remember having to learn a lot of rubbishy words which was very difficult. When I first heard what the part was about, I thought: Oh, well, I don't know what the hell this is about, but it sounds fun.

'I remember one scene in particular. I was in the kitchen as usual and while Reggie was talking to me I was cutting the head off a chicken. I'm a bit squeamish at the best of times and it made me feel sick!'

(Jo Brady)

Sue Nicholls

JOAN GREENGROSS

Joan was Reggie's loyal secretary at Sunshine Desserts, and had been for eight years when the Reggie Perrin saga began. In many ways she was the archetypal secretary: efficient, dependable, orderly, unflappable and protective of her unpredictable boss. But simmering just below the surface was an intense sexuality and passion. She found Reggie very attractive and was not afraid to reveal her feelings.

To Reggie, his secretary was much more than someone who helped organise his day. She was a steadying influence in the chaotic world of exotic ices and the only person he looked forward to seeing at work. Reggie constantly fantasized about Joan, was tormented every time she crossed her never-ending legs and, perhaps, felt she possessed the qualities he sought in a woman that were missing in his own wife.

Life at Sunshine Desserts was never the same for Joan after Reggie disappeared. When her former boss reappeared and opened Grot, Joan was working at the Glycero Ointment Corporation in Godalming. Reggie - fed up with the staid Miss Erith - asked Joan to become his secretary again, so long as she did not keep crossing her legs.

At the commune, Joan - sporting a new hippy image, and back with her husband Tony Webster after a brief separation - was given responsibility for music.

In the fourth series, Joan is unemployed after being replaced by a 22-year-old bimbo, and has split from Tony, who has fled to New Zealand.

Before joining the rest of the cast on location in Buckinghamshire, Sue Nicholls had to watch one of the old episodes to remind herself how she played Joan. 'I was nervous about playing the character again after so long,' she says. 'Although I've played Audrey in Coronation Street for 17 years, I wasn't given a long-term contract until 1984. But ever since then I've had to dedicate all my time to playing her. The only disadvantage of spending so much of one's life with one character is you get scared whenever you're asked to do anything else.'

Sue was delighted when she heard the BBC were making another series of Reggie Perrin. 'I was frantic to do it because I'd been part of the series from the beginning, and got very sad when it looked as if things wouldn't work out because of conflicting work schedules between Reggie and The Street. The thought of watching it and seeing someone else playing Joan was unthinkable. Luckily, everything's worked out, and although I can't appear in every episode, I'll be in four of them.'

Although Sue had bought David Nobbs's new novel, *The Legacy of Reginald Perrin*, before she knew the series was going ahead, she could not find time to read it. But her husband, Mark Eden (who played former *Coronation Street* bad guy Alan Bradley), did have and classed it as 'brilliant'. 'Mark's not an easy person to please because he writes himself, but he found it extremely funny. Then one morning I woke up at 5 o'clock and couldn't get back to sleep so decided to pick up the scripts – which had arrived the day before. To get me laughing at five in the morning is extremely difficult, but the scripts were wonderful and I couldn't stop.

'But it doesn't feel like 20 years since we first started Reggie Perrin,' says Sue, 'probably because it's repeated so much. It's one of the most memorable jobs I've ever done, and for my agent as well because he negotiated the contract from his hospital bed, where he was waiting to have an operation!'

Sue remembers her interview with John Howard Davies – who produced the pilot – because of its unusual venue. 'I was touring

Sue Nicholls as Joan Greengross in Series Four

in *Alfie* with Dennis Waterman and my agent called to tell me the BBC wanted to see me about playing the secretary in Reggie Perrin, but that I would have to go to London.

'As I had a show that particular evening I flew down. But being a bit scared of leaving the airport just in case I missed the flight back, John Howard Davies agreed to interview me at Heathrow Airport! Everything went well and he offered me the job.'

Fans of Reggie Perrin and of the character Joan still write to Sue saying how much they enjoyed the show and liked seeing her playing Joan. 'It's amazing. There's one fan in Australia who's written to me regularly over the years about Joan, and I hold on to letters like that because they're important.'

Sue - whose father, Lord Harmar-Nicholls, was a Tory MP for nearly 25 years and one of the first Euro MPs – did not come from a theatrical background, but was influenced, somewhat, by her grandmother. 'I danced and sang like most little girls, and while my grandmother played the piano I entertained the family with my own performances.'

Born in Walsall, Sue was educated at boarding school. Set to study languages at Oxford, she changed her mind at the last minute to try her luck at acting.

'My elocution teacher at school told me all about drama school and I decided acting was for me. Luckily, my parents loved the theatre so when I mooted my plans to them they were pleased.'

Sue trained at RADA for two years. Upon leaving, she got a job in weekly rep as a lowly ASM, looking after the likes of John Inman and Trevor Bannister, who both found fame in *Are You Being Served?* Gradually she progressed from bit parts to leading characters around the country until her 1964 TV debut in *Crossroads* playing waitress Marilyn Gates.

Reginald Perrin

'I was in rep at Weston-super-Mare at the time, but was fortunate enough to have a week off. So I nipped up to Birmingham to audition for what turned out to be the part of Jill, Meg's daughter.'

Sue did not get the job – the part being offered to Jane Rossington instead – which was fortuitous in one way because Reg Watson, the producer, thought she was ideal for the part of cocky waitress Marilyn.

During the four years Sue was at the motel she released a hit single 'Where Will You Be?' which reached number 17 in the charts in July 1968. 'It was rare in those days for actors to release records and thanks to the show it was a success, although the music papers slated it because they thought the song rather twee. I made a follow-up – again written by Tony Hatch – but by that time I'd left the show and the record flopped.'

Sue returned to the theatre doing pantos and summer seasons, including 13 weeks on Bournemouth Pier with Bob Monkhouse, while continuing to appear on TV, such as *Play for Today*, with Robert Powell; *Dixon of Dock Green; The Professionals;* the barmaid Big Brenda in *Not On Your Nellie;* Jim Davidson's neighbour in *Up the Elephant and Round the Castle;* Nadia Popov in *Rentaghost; The Duchess of Duke Street; Doctor on the Go and Heartland* – to name but a few.

After Sue's brief excursion away from Weatherfield life, she will once more concentrate solely on Audrey, now that filming has finished on *The Legacy of Reginald Perrin.* 'But I'll always be grateful for having the chance to play Joan again because I love the character, I love the cast and for the second time around it's been such fun!'

Sue Nicholls in 1971

SERIES FOUR:

Overview of Series

EPISODE 1:

After nearly 20 years apart all the characters are brought together by the death of Reggie Perrin. After attending the funeral they are all summoned to Geraldine Hackstraw's office – the solicitor dealing with Reggie's estate – to hear the reading of the will. Everyone is left a million pounds on the condition that they carry out an absurd act – the level of absurdity to be judged by Ms Hackstraw.

Reggie's entourage gather to pay their respects

Jimmy, Elizabeth and the solicitor in charge of Reggie's estate, Geraldine Hackstraw

EPISODE 2:
Eager to claim their share of Reggie's fortune, everyone embarks on individual attempts at absurdity, but fail dismally. They decide to pool their resources but working as a group is less than effective until they adopt Jimmy as their unlikely leader!

EPISODE 3:
Joan introduces a new face to the group. Hank, Joan's new boyfriend, is voted into

the team in their quest for absurdity. Deciding to form the Bloodless Revolution of Senior Citizens and the Occupationally Rejected (BROSCOR), everyone sets out on a recruitment drive for new members. Ms Hackstraw, meanwhile, receives constant invites to dinner from certain members of the team eager for her affections.

EPISODE 4:
A dearth of ideas dampens morale until Jimmy – trying to pass Elizabeth's ideas off as his own, with her consent, of course – suggests splitting into two units: one as a

Doc Horsley, Tom Patterson and C.J. are in need of inspiration

Think Tank, the other as a Policy Research Unit. Things get a bit confusing when Jimmy decides being the leader means he has to be on both units. Romance is in the air once again for Tom and Linda, who try rekindling their love for each other. C.J. begins acting suspiciously.

EPISODE 5:
C.J. is not himself – or so everybody thinks

Joan with her new boyfriend Hank

Tom and Linda remarry

Ms Hackstraw receives solicitous attentions from Doc Horsley and C.J.

– because he is being incredibly nice. Suspicious of his motives, Jimmy nominates Tom and David to keep an eye on C.J. to find out what is behind his sudden change of mood. BROSCOR gets its first recruit. The double wedding of Tom and Linda, and Hank and Joan takes place, and David unfortunately drinks too much at the reception.

EPISODE 6:
After the wedding reception, David – nursing a hangover – worries that he may have blown the security surrounding the group's idea for taking over the Government. Jimmy has an inspiration that becomes extremely complex; he also begins a relationship with Ms Hackstraw.

EPISODE 7:
It is the day of the revolution and thousands of OAPs converge on London in coaches hijacked by the team for their bloodless revolution. As well as marching on Whitehall to take over the Government, the team nominate Jimmy to oust Angela Rippon from her seat on the national news in order to deliver an appeal on TV in support of the revolution. Sadly, it seems as if the authorities have been tipped off and prevent the OAPs from descending on

The OAPs converge on London

Parliament. It is also judgment day: Ms Hackstraw gives her verdict on the team's attempts at being absurd, and on the future of her relationship with Jimmy.

After being on exclusive contract to Yorkshire TV for years, producer Gareth Gwenlan enticed David Nobbs back to the BBC by offering him an open-ended commission: he was free to write a comedy series about anything he liked. But when David told Gareth what he wanted to do the producer's heart sank.

'I'd always kept in touch with David and gradually we became good friends. Every time his Yorkshire contract came up for renewal, I'd say to him: "You're not going to sign again, are you?" at which point he'd be offered more money and sign,' says Gareth.

'Then about two years ago he told me there had been a change of management at Yorkshire and no mention had been made of a new contract. So I jumped in and although I hadn't spoken to my head of department I took it upon myself to commission David to write a comedy series. He was happy and decided to go away and think of an idea.'

Two weeks later, David contacted Gareth. A meeting was arranged to discuss his plans. 'The moment David walked into my office I could tell he was enthused about his idea. However, I was initially a little worried when he told me he wanted to write a further series of Reggie Perrin. The thought of reviving it wasn't a decision to be taken lightly. But to be honest, it didn't take much to make me realise it could work. There was never any question of even trying to replace Leonard because that certainly wouldn't have worked, and anyway David's idea was dealing with his legacy.'

Gareth commissioned David Nobbs to write the first episode which also meant he could complete the first four chapters of his novel. 'He used to fax pages of the book to me and as soon as they arrived it was perfectly clear that David was on top form.'

Running deeply throughout the previous novels and TV series had been a rich vein of truth: aspects of society are explored through absurdities and ridiculous situations. First we saw the tedious routine of life; then a glance at a world producing and selling useless items, and in the third series a desire to make the world a better place in which to live.

For the fourth, David Nobbs has focused once again on a current theme. 'It seems to me as if industry is losing all its experienced workers through redundancy and early retirement and is oblivious to the fact,' he says.

'In the book and, of course, the TV series Doc Morrisey dreams up the idea of young-age pensions. Everyone has a pension between 18 and 28 and instead of working they learn about life. At the other end of the age scale people don't have pensions but have job security instead; they don't find themselves redundant and on the scrap heap.'

Geraldine Hackstraw

When David began working on his new idea, he had little alternative but to kill Reggie off. With Leonard Rossiter dying in 1984, David sent Reggie to his maker by having a billboard – advertising the actual insurance company with which he was insured – land on him after it had been blown over during a storm.

To qualify as beneficiaries of his will all the old crew, with the exception of Tony Webster, have to carry out an absurd act.

Reggie's final years were largely uneventful – hardly surprising after such a crazy life – and rather sad. 'There was nothing further for him to do so he just lived in Leibinitz Avenue until he died,' explains David Nobbs.

'He was exhausted after doing so much but disappointed to find that he hadn't really achieved anything with his various rebellions because he ended back at square one. But he always hoped someone would carry on his absurdities which is why he has written his will in this way.'

Before filming began sceptics were already questioning how a new series without the late, great Leonard Rossiter would work, as Gareth Gwenlan was only too aware. 'It's obviously a valid question. How do you do Hamlet without the Prince? The answer is simple: you market it differently. There are constant references to Reggie – as one would expect – and the solicitor, Ms Hackstraw, acts in many ways as the mouthpiece for Reggie because she has to judge whether the absurdities warrant the pay-out from the will.

'Len was obviously the driver in the previous three series, but the other main characters all got their fair share of laughs. And it was perfectly clear from the new scripts that there was more than enough humour to justify the fourth series even without the brilliance of Leonard Rossiter.'

David Nobbs shares Gareth's views.

'Although Leonard was an exceptional actor and played a massive part in making Reggie Perrin so successful, we have to forget about him for the new series and concentrate on all the other characters because they're funny enough.

'Geoffrey Palmer is now a much-loved star where he was a supporting actor in the original three series. Sue Nicholls is a popular *Coronation Street* actress, and there's new blood with the likes of Patricia Hodge, who needs no introduction.'

In adjusting to the length of time since we last saw the characters, David has very delicately reshaped some of their personalities and mannerisms. While C.J. is as severe and booming as ever and Doc Morrisey the same ol' bungling but likeable fool, the passing years have increased David's self-confidence slightly. As a result, he stutters less and is rather more loquacious. Jimmy's been out of uniform so long he uses the clipped military lingo a little less, and Tom is certainly less pompous.

Besides most of the original cast *The Legacy of Reginald Perrin* introduces several new faces to the series including Michael Fenton-Stevens, playing Joan's new fiancé Hank, and Patricia as solicitor Geraldine Hackstraw, who was David Nobbs's first choice for playing the character.

'David had worked with her before,' explains Gareth Gwenlan, 'and wanted her to play the part. I was interested in Patricia playing Geraldine as well, but the trouble was she was heavily committed to the theatre when we began thinking

about casting. Anyway, I sent her the scripts and within a few days I had a phone call from her agent saying she would love to do it and would find a way of being available.'

As far as Patricia Hodge was concerned she had no intentions of allowing other work commitments prevent her from playing Geraldine. 'I had worked on David's *Rich Tea and Sympathy* for Yorkshire TV in 1991 and he said then that he wanted to work with me again. About 18 months ago he came to see me in *The Prime of Miss Jean Brodie* and told me he was writing a sequel to Reggie Perrin and wanted me to play the part of the solicitor. I didn't think anything more of it until Gareth Gwenlan's office called asking me to play Geraldine – it was as if it was always meant to be. I love David's work so much I would never have hesitated in accepting the part, even without reading the scripts.'

Patricia hopes viewers and critics will view the new series without any preconceived ideas. 'The obvious statement for people to make will be to point the finger and ask how it can be done without Leonard. But the good thing about this series is that it has a life of its own and has nothing to do with any previous incarnations. It is the life after Reggie which is focused on.

'The programme has a clutch of first-rate actors who together are like a sublime repertory company made in heaven,' she says. 'The shorthand they have

Geoffrey Palmer as Jimmy with Pauline Yates as Elizabeth Perrin

Patricia Hodge, who plays Geraldine Hackstraw in Series Four

between them – even 18 years on – is unbelievable. During the read-through I just sat with my mouth open because they switched into their roles as if they'd never been away from it.

'Leonard was a genius but he had a particular form of energy that would dominate whatever he was in. Now all these other actors are able to flourish, and the microscope can be placed on them to see what they're up to.'

Patricia is proud to be associated with the new Perrin series. 'My reward in Reggie is being part of this wonderful company. Geraldine is by far the straightest of all the characters in the series and I could have mugged her because all the other characters are larger than life. But I knew that wouldn't be a good idea because you need a catalyst, a sober voice in the heart of the series around which revolves utter madness – and that's Geraldine.

'Another great thing about it is that *The Legacy of Reginald Perrin* is more than just a sitcom. It pushes the boundaries of comedy into a different area: you can laugh wildly but it can also be a little tragic or sad. And that's one of the reasons I like David's writing so much. He writes comically about human fallibility and idiosyncrasies, but also manages to write the most brilliant social document at any given moment: a perspective on exactly where society is at any time. I think it's amazing that he focused on the question of youth being empowered and the old aged and redundant having no focal point. I think we'll look back in 50 years time and say: "Gosh! This series gives us more insight into where human attitudes were at that time than any of the history books."'

Hank, meanwhile, who is almost a direct replacement for Tony Webster, marries Joan during the course of the series, and helps inject an additional freshness into the programme. 'He starts off by being white-haired and looking haggard,' says David. 'He looks 60 but is actually only 39; it is just that he works on a futures desk in the City and is burnt out. He is finally made redundant because he's told there is no future in futures, and is recruited to help with the bloodless revolution with his catchphrase "Wicked!"'

Michael Fenton-Stevens believes he may have his hair to thank for getting the part of Hank. 'The interesting thing about the character is that he recovers his age during the run of the series. He turns from appearing 60 in the beginning to his late 30s by the end which is quite a challenge for the make-up department. But I think my long grey hair could have been one of the reasons I was offered the part.

'I'd worked with Gareth Gwenlan before on *Only Fools and Horses* and Geoffrey Palmer on a series of sketches for Comic Relief but apart from that I hadn't worked with anyone else from the cast,' he says.

'What is good about the series, and was the case in the other three, is that many of the characters, including Hank, are an important part of the assemblage and responsible for moving the story along. So much of the script is group discussion which is unusual and probably the most difficult writing to pull off because everybody has a reasonable amount to play.'

Michael was an original fan of the series, but did not set out to be an actor himself. 'I trained as a lawyer and fell into revue with university friends. After a successful performance at Edinburgh we were offered a radio pilot for Radio 4, so I dropped law after qualifying and pursued acting.'

Comedy revue has featured heavily in his career. He has appeared in eight series for Radio 4 with a company called Radioactive, together with four other actors including Angus Deayton and Geoffrey Perkins, now Head of Comedy at the BBC. He has also made several TV appearances, his break arriving with BBC2's *KYTV*.

But Michael is proud to be involved in the new series of Reggie. 'It's still such a popular show. I know lots of people, such as my younger brother, who remember vast swathes of the original series, especially all the characters and their roles.'

As far as Michael is concerned, reviving the series has been a good idea. 'It's looking at all the characters 20 years later. It's partly an exploration to see how everyone

has survived without Reggie, but, of course, his influence is there all the time because his will reunites them all and sets them a challenge.

'In many ways their lives have been fairly static without him and he comes back into their lives through the will to set them off on course again. I certainly believe the series will be a success.'

Filming has now finished and fans everywhere eagerly await the screening this autumn. David Nobbs is quietly confident that the series will be well received.

'It's all gone terribly well and the omens are good, but we'll just have to wait and see. It has certainly been fun seeing the series come together. I was astounded when I went along to watch the filming because everybody was excellent. John Barron was stunning and in my view better now than when he did the originals. His voice is so powerful he dominates just like the old C.J. John Horsley doesn't seem to have aged and is just as lively as he was 20 years ago. And seeing Geoffrey Palmer in drag as a transvestite was hilarious – everyone was falling about laughing!'

Hopefully, the series will attract a whole new audience but both David and Gareth have resisted the temptation to recommend transmitting repeats before its launch.

'Gareth and I had long talks about whether it would be a good idea to screen some of the original episodes and we've decided not to recommend an airing. We think there will be such interest in the new series that we'll squander it with repeats.

'I think new viewers will understand that this chap has died and left a condition in his will. If they don't know who Reggie is they'll follow the story from that point. But, of course, many younger viewers will know about Reggie Perrin from their parents or friends.'

We wait in anticipation.

CAST AND CREW LISTS

CREW LIST – SERIES 1, 2 & 3

PRODUCER: John Howard Davies (pilot episode only)
Gareth Gwenlan
PRODUCTION ASSISTANT. Brian Jones (pilot)
John B Hobbs (series 1, 2 & 3)
FILM CAMERAMAN: Reg Pope (series 1 & 2)
Alec Curtis (series 3)
FILM EDITOR: Chris Lovett (pilot)
Graham Walker (series 1) Bill Harris (series 2)
Dan Rae (series 3)
SOUND RECORDIST: Richard Chamberlain (pilot)
Basil Harris (series 1) Bill Wild (series 2)
Rodney Bond (series 3)
STUDIO SOUND: Laurie Taylor (series 1)
Jeff Booth/Malcolm Johnson (series 2)
Jack Sudic (series 3)
COSTUME: June Hudson (pilot)
Janet Tharby/Joyce Mortlock (series 1)
Janet Tharby/Dennis Brack (series 2)
Christian Dyall (series 3)
MAKE-UP: Dawn Alcock (series 1)
Christine Whitney (series 2)
Frances Needham (series 3)
LIGHTING: Jimmy Purdie (pilot)
Brian Clemett/Ron Koplick (series 1)
Derek Slee/John Dixon (series 2)
John Dixon (series 3)
DESIGNER: Graham Oakley (pilot)
Lesley Bremness/Barbara Gosnold (series 1)
Jon Pusey/Pamela Lambooy (series 2)
Gloria Clayton/Pamela Lambooy (series 3)
MUSIC: Ronnie Hazlehurst
GRAPHIC DESIGNER: Stewart Austin (series 1 & 2, episodes 7)

CAST LIST
ACTORS PRESENT IN EACH OF THE 21 EPISODES
Leonard Rossiter: Reginald Perrin
Pauline Yates: Elizabeth Perrin

OTHER CAST MEMBERS – SERIES 1
EPISODE 1 (PILOT) Original Transmission Date: 8/9/76
John Barron: C.J.
Sue Nicholls: Joan Greengross
John Horsley: Doc Morrisey
Trevor Adams: Tony Webster
Bruce Bould: David Harris-Jones
Roland Macleod: Morris Coates
Jacki Piper: Esther Pigeon
Terence Conoley: Peter Cartwright
Norman Mitchell: Ron Napier
Ray Marioni: Waiter

EPISODE 2 Original Transmission Date: 15/9/76
Sue Nicholls: Joan Greengross
Trevor Adams: Tony Webster
Bruce Bould: David Harris-Jones

John Horsley: Doc Morrisey
John Barron: C.J.
Geoffrey Palmer: Jimmy
Sally-Jane Spencer: Linda
Tim Preece: Tom
Terence Conoley: Peter Cartwright
Penny Leatherbarrow: Tea Lady
Abigail Morgan: Jocasta
Robert Hillier: Adam

EPISODE 3 Original Transmission Date: 22/9/76
Sue Nicholls: Joan Greengross
Tim Preece: Tom
Geoffrey Palmer: Jimmy
David Warwick: Mark

EPISODE 4 Original Transmission Date: 29/9/76
Sue Nicholls: Joan Greengross
John Barron: C.J.
Trevor Adams: Tony Webster
Bruce Bould: David Harris-Jones
John Horsley: Doc Morrisey
Terence Conoley: Peter Cartwright
Tim Barrett: Mr Campbell-Lewiston
Virginia Balfour: Davina Letts-Wilkinson
Dorothy Frere: Mrs C.J.
Tony Sympson: Uncle Percy Spillinger

EPISODE 5 Original Transmission Date: 6/10/76
Sue Nicholls: Joan Greengross
John Barron: C.J.
Trevor Adams: Tony Webster
Bruce Bould. David Harris-Jones
John Horsley: Doc Morrisey
Terence Conoley: Peter Cartwright
Dennis Ramsden: Dr Hump
Tenniel Evans: Elwyn Watkins
John Rudling: Bill

EPISODE 6 Original Transmission Date: 13/10/76
John Barron: C.J.
Bruce Bould: David Harris-Jones
Trevor Adams: Tony Webster
Sally-Jane Spencer: Linda
Anne Cunningham: Jean Timpkins
Ken Wynne: Mr Deacon
Hilary Manson: Mrs Deaconl
Charmian May: Miss Pershore
Roger Brierley: Mr Thorneycroft
Pamela Manson: Barmaid
John Forbes-Robertson: Henry Possett
David Millet: Landlord
Vi Kane: Neighbour
Hamilton McLeod: Waiter
Bob Sutherland: Major

EPISODE 7 Original Transmission Date: 20/10/76
Sue Nicholls: Joan Greengross
John Barron: C.J.
Trevor Adams: Tony Webster
Bruce Bould: David Harris-Jones
Geoffrey Palmer: Jimmy
Sally-Jane Spencer: Linda

Tim Preece: Tom
Charmian May: Miss Pershore
Gerald Sim: Vicar
David Warwick: Mark
John Forbes-Robertson: Henry Possett
Dorothy Frere: Mrs C.J.
Peter MacKriel: Waiter

SERIES 2
EPISODE 1 Original Transmission Date: 21/9/77
Sue Nicholls: Joan Greengross
John Barron: C.J.
Trevor Adams: Tony Webster
Bruce Bould: David Harris-Jones
John Horsley: Doc Morrisey
Geoffrey Palmer: Jimmy
Sally-Jane Spencer: Linda
Tim Preece: Tom
David Rowley: Owen Lewis
Ken Barker: G.P.O. Engineer
Derek Deadman: Man at telephone box

EPISODE 2 Original Transmission Date: 28/9/77
Sue Nicholls: Joan Greengross
John Barron: C.J.
Trevor Adams: Tony Webster
Bruce Bould: Davis Harris-Jones
Sally-Jane Spencer: Linda
Tim Preece: Tom
Glynn Edwards: Mr Pelham
Terence Conoley: Peter Cartwright
Christopher Lawrence: House buyer
Ralph Watson: Clerk at Labour Exchange
Helen Bernat: Girl at bus stop

EPISODE 3 Original Transmission Date: 5/10/77
Sue Nicholls: Joan Greengross
John Barron: C.J.
Trevor Adams: Tony Webster
Bruce Bould: David Harris-Jones
Geoffrey Palmer: Jimmy
Sally-Jane Spencer: Linda
Tim Preece: Tom
Glynn Edwards: Mr Pelham

EPISODE 4 Original Transmission Date: 12/10/77
Sue Nicholls: Joan Greengross
John Barron: C.J.
Trevor Adams: Tony Webster
Bruce Bould: David Harris-Jones
Sally-Jane Spencer: Linda
Tim Preece: Tom
Roland Macleod: Morris Coates
Jacki Piper: Esther Pigeon
Joan Blackham: Miss Erith
Terence Conoley: Peter Cartwright
Edward Dentith: Mr Milford
Michael Bilton: Wine-buyer
Cynthia Etherington: Housewife
Del Derrick: Well-dressed man
Beatrice Shaw: Elderly lady
Gilly Flower: Woman with fur

EPISODE 5 Original Transmission Date: 19/10/77
Sue Nicholls: Joan Greengross
John Barron: C.J.
Trevor Adams: Tony Webster
Bruce Bould: David Harris-Jones
Joan Blackham: Miss Erith

EPISODE 6 Original Transmission Date: 26/10/77
Sue Nicholls: Joan Greengross
John Barron: C.J.
Trevor Adams: Tony Webster
Bruce Bould: David Harris-Jones
John Horsley: Doc Morrisey
Geoffrey Palmer: Jimmy
Sally-Jane Spencer: Linda
Tim Preece.: Tom
Derry Power: Seamus Finnegan
Sheila Bernette: Gladys
Ken Morley: Arthur
Robert Hillier: Adam
Abigail Morgan: Jocasta

EPISODE 7 Original Transmission Date: 2/11/77
Sue Nicholls: Joan Greengross
John Barron: C.J.
Trevor Adams: Tony Webster
Bruce Bould: David Harris-Jones
Geoffrey Palmer: Jimmy
John Horsley: Doc Morrisey
Sally-Jane Spencer: Linda
Tim Preece: Tom
Timothy Carlton: Colin Pillock
Blain Fairman: Sheridan Honeydew
Neville Barber: Peregrine Trembleby
Keith Smith: Mr Lisburn
David Rowlands: Mr Herbert

SERIES 3
EPISODE 1 Original Transmission Date: 29/11/78
Sue Nicholls: Joan Greengross
John Barron: C.J.
John Horsley: Doc Morrisey
Trevor Adams: Tony Webster
Bruce Bould: David Harris-Jones
Sally-Jane Spencer: Linda
Leslie Schofield: Tom
Theresa Watson: Prue Harris-Jones
Brian Coburn: Big man in bank
George Tovey: Little man in bank
David Hanson: Bank clerk
Leslie Rhodes: Barman
Ali Baba: Indian in park
Robert Hillier: Adam
Abigail Morgan: Jocasta

EPISODE 2 Original Transmission Date: 6/12/78
Sue Nicholls: Joan Greengross
John Barron: C.J.
John Horsley: Doc Morrisey
Geoffrey Palmer: Jimmy
Trevor Adams: Tony Webster
Bruce Bould: David Harris-Jones
Theresa Watson: Prue Harris-Jones

Sally-Jane Spencer: Linda
Leslie Schofield: Tom
Joseph Brady: McBlane
Arnold Peters: Mr Penfold
Joyce Windsor: Mrs Hollies
James Warrior: Mr Babbacombe
Stewart Quentin Holmes: Passer-by on canal towpath

EPISODE 3 Original Transmission Date: 13/12/78
Sue Nicholls: Joan Greengross
John Barron: C.J.
John Horsley: Doc Morrisey
Geoffrey Palmer: Jimmy
Trevor Adams: Tony Webster
Bruce Bould: David Harris-Jones
Theresa Watson: Prue Harris-Jones
Sally-Jane Spencer: Linda
Leslie Schofield: Tom
Glynn Edwards: Mr Pelham
Leslie Sands: Thruxton Appleby
Frederick Jaeger: Bernard Trilling
Ronald Pember: Arthur Noblet
Sally Lahee: Hilary Meadows

EPISODE 4 Original Transmission Date: 20/12/78
Sue Nicholls: Joan Greengross
John Barron: C.J.
John Horsley: Doc Morrisey
Geoffrey Palmer: Jimmy
Trevor Adams: Tony Webster
Bruce Bould: David Harris-Jones
Theresa Watson: Prue Harris-Jones
Sally-Jane Spencer: Linda
Leslie Schofield: Tom
Joseph Brady: McBlane
Robert Gillespie: Mr Dent
Peter Schofield: Mr Winstanley
David Ellison: Factory owner
Bunny May: Insurance salesman
Janet Davies: Ethel Merman
Peter Hill: Edwards
Michael Segal: Mr Jenkins
Andrew Johns: Mr Pennell
Peter Roberts: Youth
Frank Baker: Shy vet

EPISODE 5 Original Transmission Date: 10/1/79
Sue Nicholls: Joan Greengross
John Barron: C.J.
John Horsley: Doc Morrisey
Geoffrey Palmer: Jimmy
Trevor Adams: Tony Webster
Bruce Bould: David Harris-Jones
Theresa Watson: Prue Harris-Jones
Sally-Jane Spencer: Linda
Leslie Schofield: Tom
Joseph Brady: McBlane
Terence Alexander: Clive 'Lofty' Anstruther
Hilary Tindall: Deborah Swaffham
Timothy Carlton: Colin Pillock
Vincent Brimble: Glenn Higgins
Gordon Case: Johnson
Frank Baker: Shy vet

Kenneth Watson: Superintendant
Leslie Glazer: Merchant banker

EPISODE 6 Original Transmission Date: 17/1/79
Sue Nicholls: Joan Greengross
John Barron: C.J.
John Horsley: Doc Morrisey
Geoffrey Palmer: Jimmy
Trevor Adams: Tony Webster
Bruce Bould: David Harris-Jones
Theresa Watson: Prue Harris-Jones
Sally-Jane Spencer: Linda
Leslie Schofield: Tom
Joseph Brady: McBlane
Derry Power: Seamus Finnegan
Joan Peart: Mrs E Blythe-Erpingham
Jonathan Fryer: Landlord
Leslie Adams: Driver

EPISODE 7 Original Transmission Date: 24/1/79
Sue Nicholls: Joan Greengross
John Barron: C.J.
John Horsley: Doc Morrisey
Geoffrey Palmer: Jimmy
Trevor Adams: Tony Webster
Bruce Bould: David Harris-Jones
Theresa Watson: Prue Harris-Jones
Sally-Jane Spencer: Linda
Leslie Schofield: Tom
John Quayle: Mr Fennel
Linda Cunningham: Iris Hoddle
Terence Woodfield: Muscroft
David Sparks: Rosewall

CREW LIST – SERIES 4
PRODUCER/DIRECTOR: Gareth Gwenlan
PRODUCTION MANAGER: Amita Lochab
TRAINEE DIRECTOR: Murray Peterson
PROODUCTION ASSISTANT: Caroline Gardener
PRODUCTION SECRETARY: Caren Williams
ASSISTANT FLOOR MANAGER: Christine Crow
FLOOR ASSISTANT: Caroline Caley
DESIGNER: David Buckingham
RT DIRECTOR: Richard Hogan
PROPERTIES BUYER: Ian Tully
COSTUME DESIGNER: Robin Stubbs
MAKE-UP DESIGNER: Kerin Parfitt
LIGHTING DIRECTOR: Duncan Brown
STUDIO RESOURCE MANAGER: Michael Langley-Evans
SOUND SUPERVISOR: John Downes
DEPUTY SOUND SUPERVISOR: Dave Howell
VISION MIXER: Heather Gilder
CAMERA SUPERVISOR: Gerry Tivers
EDITOR: Chris Wadsworth

CAST LIST – SERIES 4
EPISODE 1
Geoffrey Palmer: Jimmy
Patricia Hodge: Geraldine Hackstraw
Pauline Yates: Elizabeth
John Barron: C.J

John Horsley: Doc Morrisey
Sue Nicholls: Joan Greengross
Tim Preece: Tom
Sally-Jane Spencer: Linda
Bruce Bould: David Harris-Jones
Theresa Watson: Prue Harris-Jones
Gerald Sim: Vicar
Paul McDowell: Higgins

EPISODE 2
Geoffrey Palmer: Jimmy
Patricia Hodge: Geraldine Hackstraw
Pauline Yates: Elizabeth
John Barron: C.J.
John Horsley: Doc Morrisey
Tim Preece: Tom
Sally-Jane Spencer: Linda
Bruce Bould: David Harris-Jones
Theresa Watson: Prue Harris-Jones
Alan David: Brian Deacon
Oliver Pierre: Napoleon
Rosalind Adler: Receptionist

EPISODE 3
Geoffrey Palmer: Jimmy
Patricia Hodge: Geraldine Hackstraw
Pauline Yates: Elizabeth
John Barron: C.J
John Horsley: Doc Morrisey
Sue Nicholls: Joan Greengross
Tim Preece: Tom
Sally-Jane Spencer: Linda
Bruce Bould: David Harris-Jones
Theresa Watson: Prue Harris-Jones
Michael Fenton-Stevens: Hank
Daniel Pageon: Head waiter
Fanny Carby: Senior citizen
Dick Ward: Coach driver
Eileen Bell: Retired cleaner
Roy Heather: Biscuit man
Oliver Bradshaw: Elderly judge
Joan Linder: Old woman
Laura Jackson: Receptionist
Peter Stockbridge: Prostate
Anthony Douse: Male chiropodist
Jean Trend: Female chiropodist

EPISODE 4
Geoffrey Palmer: Jimmy
Patricia Hodge: Geraldine Hackstraw
Pauline Yates: Elizabeth
John Barron: C.J.
John Horsley: Doc Morrisey
Tim Preece: Tom
Sally-Jane Spencer: Linda
Bruce Bould: David Harris-Jones
Theresa Watson: Prue Harris-Jones
Michael Fenton-Stevens: Hank
Brenda Cowling: Mrs Wren

EPISODE 5
Geoffrey Palmer: Jimmy
Patricia Hodge: Geraldine Hackstraw
Pauline Yates: Elizabeth
John Barron: C.J.
John Horsley: Doc Morrisey
Sue Nicholls: Joan Greengross
Tim Preece: Tom
Sally-Jane Spencer: Linda
Bruce Bould: David Harris-Jones
Theresa Watson: Prue Harris-Jones
James Bannon: Morton Radstock
David Ryall: Welton Ormsby
Michael Fenton-Stevens: Hank
Roger Brierley: Alan Maseby-Smythe
David Bark-Jones: Adam Perrin
Penelope Woodman: Angie
Peter Penry-Jones: Tim Ripley

EPISODE 6
Geoffrey Palmer: Jimmy
Patricia Hodge: Geraldine Hackstraw
Pauline Yates: Elizabeth
John Barron: C.J.
John Horsley: Doc Morrisey
Tim Preece: Tom
Sally-Jane Spencer: Linda
Bruce Bould: David Harris-Jones
Theresa Watson: Prue Harris-Jones
Michael Fenton-Stevens: Hank
David Ryall: Welton Ormsby
James Bannon: Morton Radstock
David Bark-Jones: Adam Perrin
Penelope Woodman: Angie
Roli Okorodudu: Nurse

EPISODE 7
Geoffrey Palmer: Jimmy
Patricia Hodge: Geraldine Hackstraw
Pauline Yates: Elizabeth
John Barron: C.J.
John Horsley: Doc Morrisey
Sue Nicholls: Joan Greengross
Tim Preece: Tom
Sally-Jane Spencer: Linda
Bruce Bould: David Harris-Jones
Theresa Watson: Prue Harris-Jones
Michael Fenton-Stevens: Hank
David Ryall: Welton Ormsby
James Bannon: Morton Radstock
Roli Okorodudu: Nurse
David Barry: Coach driver 1
David McAlister: Senior police officer
Ian Peck: Police Patrolman
David Aldous: Coach driver 2
Martin Hyder: Barry Benskin
Fionnuala Ellwood: Carol Benskin
Jean Grover: Mildred
Toby Longworth: Radio D.J.
Angela Rippon: Herself